COS

The idea of cosmopolitanism is increasingly in circulation both in the social sciences and in the language of everyday life. There is, however, much uncertainty about what it means, what it refers to and what role it plays in social scientific thinking.

In this book Robert Fine explores the concept of cosmopolitanism, its contribution to critical thought, and its application to a number of pressing political issues: taming global marketisation, resisting the resurgence of nationalism and fundamentalism, constructing transnational forms of political community, enhancing the role of international law and human rights, prosecuting crimes against humanity and assessing the legitimacy of humanitarian military intervention. He explores the idea of cosmopolitanism both as a description of social reality and as a key element in the life of the modern mind.

Cosmopolitanism offers an innovative discussion of the social, legal and political dimensions of the cosmopolitan turn in the social sciences. It should be of interest to students and researchers in the fields of social theory, sociology, political theory, cultural studies, international relations and law.

Robert Fine is Professor of Sociology at the University of Warwick, UK. He has been engaged in theoretical research in the areas of natural law and social theory, cosmopolitan social theory and more empirical research in the areas of racism, anti-Semitism and nationalism.

KEY IDEAS

SERIES EDITOR: PETER HAMILTON, THE OPEN UNIVERSITY, MILTON KEYNES

Designed to compliment the successful *Key Sociologists*, this series covers the main concepts, issues, debates, and controversies in sociology and the social sciences. The series aims to provide authoritative essays on central topics of social science, such as community, power, work, sexuality, inequality, benefits and ideology, class, family, etc. Books adopt a strong 'individual' line, as critical essays rather than literature surveys, offering lively and original treatments of their subject matter. The books will be useful to students and teachers of sociology, political science, economics, psychology, philosophy, and geography.

Citizenship
KEITH FAULKS

Class
STEPHEN EDGELL

Communi
GERARD DELANTY

Consumption
ROBERT BOCOCK

Globalization - second edition
MALCOLM WATERS

Lifestyle
DAVID CHANEY

Mass Media
PIERRE SORLIN

Moral Panics
KENNETH THOMPSON

Old Age
JOHN VINCENT

Postmodernity
BARRY SMART

Racism – second edition
ROBERT MILES AND
MALCOLM BROWN

Risk
DEBORAH LUPTON

Sexuality – second edition
JEFFREY WEEKS

Social Capital
JOHN FIELD

Transgression
CHRIS JENKS

The Virtual
ROB SHIELDS

Social Identity – second edition
RICHARD JENKINS

Culture – second edition
CHRIS JENKS

Human Rights
ANTHONY WOODIWISS

Childhood – second edition
CHRIS JENKS

Cosmopolitanism
ROBERT FINE

COSMOPOLITANISM

Robert Fine

Routledge
Taylor & Francis Group

LONDON AND NEW YORK

First published 2007 by Routledge
2 Park Square, Milton Park, Abingdon, Oxon, OX14 4RN

Simultaneously published in the USA and Canada by Routledge 270
Madison Avenue, New York, NY 10016

Routledge is an imprint of the Taylor & Francis Group
© 2007 Robert Fine

Typeset in Garamond and Scala by Prepress Projects Ltd, Perth, UK

Printed and bound in Great Britain by MPG Books Ltd, Bodmin

British Library Cataloguing in Publication Data
A catalogue record for this book is available from the British Library

Library of Congress Cataloging in Publication Data
Fine, Robert, 1945–
Cosmopolitanism/Robert Fine.
p. cm.
Includes bibliographical references.
1. Cosmopolitanism. I. Title.
JZ1308.F56 2007
306–dc22
2007016118

ISBN10: 0–415–39224–1 (hbk)
ISBN10: 0–415–39225–X (pbk)

ISBN13: 978–0–415–39224–2 (hbk)
ISBN13: 978–0–415–39225–9 (pbk)

To Shoshi, with love

Contents

PREFACE: TWENTY-ONE THESES ON COSMOPOLITAN SOCIAL THEORY

1 The idea of cosmopolitanism existed long before that of nationalism. It started with the ancient Greeks and has since played a pivotal part within social and political thought. In the closing years of the eighteenth century Kant wrote of the 'cosmopolitan condition' as a rational necessity linking nations together on the grounds that in the modern age 'a violation of rights in one part of the world is felt everywhere' (Kant 1991: 107–8). In the early nineteenth century Hegel declared it a matter of 'infinite importance' that 'a human being counts as such because he is a human being, not because he is a Jew, Catholic, Protestant, German, Italian, etc.' (Hegel 1991: §209R). In the mid-nineteenth century Karl Marx wrote of capitalism as a world system deeply disintegrative of nation-states and saw worldwide capitalism as the base on which the project of *human* emancipation and a science of *human* association could be built up. At the turn of the nineteenth and twentieth centuries the sociologist Emile Durkheim looked to the coming of a 'world patriotism' or cosmopolitanism in which 'societies can have their pride, not in being the greatest or the wealthiest, but in being the most just, the best organised and in possessing the best moral constitution' (Durkheim 1992: 74–5). In the 1970s the sociologist Raymond Aron wrote that the technological unification of the world under the register of 'industrialism' had become the infrastructure upon which a deeper recognition of human unity could be achieved, that 'the dialectic of universality is the mainspring of the march of history' (Aron 1972: 306) and that the 'move from a national to a human frame of reference' is the challenge facing sociology (Aron 1972: 200). Today Ulrich Beck writes of 'the cosmopolitanisation of reality' that results from the fact that humanity now faces common global risks and argues that the move from 'methodological nationalism' to 'methodological cosmopolitanism' is the key challenge facing sociology.

2 Cosmopolitan social theory is a collective endeavour to build a science of society founded on a claim to universalism. Its basic presupposition is that the human species can be understood only if it is treated as a single subject, within which all forms of difference are recognised and respected but conceptualised as internal to the substantive unity of all human beings. Universalism, based on the global reach of modernity and the ultimate unity of humankind, is both its methodological approach to understanding the world and its normative approach to changing the world.

3 Cosmopolitan social theory reconstructs the history and traditions of social theory in terms of its universalistic concept of society, the recognition of differences within a universalistic frame, and the critique of methodological and political nationalism. It stands firm against approaches to understanding and changing society grounded in nationalist, racist, sexist or anti-Semitic presuppositions. Cosmopolitan social theory is in this sense no more than social theory made mindful of its own cosmopolitan spirit.

4 Part of this book takes the form of a critical engagement with what I call the 'new cosmopolitanism' within the social sciences. I criticise the new cosmopolitanism not for being cosmopolitan but for not being cosmopolitan enough. It attaches cosmopolitanism to an already strong and confident sense of belonging (whether it is Ghanaian village society, or post-war German constitutional democracy, or the European way of life, or indeed American democracy). It leaves intact a conventional notion of belonging, in which individuals know intimately the contours of their world, and it only supplements this sense of belonging with a universal element. For me, the appeal of cosmopolitanism has to do with the idea that human beings can belong anywhere, humanity has shared predicaments and we find our community with others in exploring how these predicaments can be faced in common. Cosmopolitan social theory is at its most powerful in addressing the needs of those who are outside or on the margins of the nation.

5 I criticise the new cosmopolitanism for its claim to be new. It has to misrepresent the tradition of social theory as resolutely 'nationalist' in order to re-present itself as newly cosmopolitan.

There is a sense in which the new cosmopolitanism is not new enough. The roots of cosmopolitanism lie in the tradition of natural law theory. Kant is its best-known representative. That the new cosmopolitanism 'returns' to Kant because it has not cut its roots in natural law theory. It modernises natural law. It extends natural law. It carries the logic of natural law to its universalistic conclusion. But it remains firmly within the premises of natural law.

6   I use the term 'cosmopolitan social theory' not to indicate a wholesale rejection of the natural law tradition nor to indicate that I or anyone else has found the master key to overcoming natural law theory, but rather to call for a critical engagement with this tradition. Cosmopolitan social theory emphasises the bridge between cosmopolitanism and social theory, between the natural law origins of cosmopolitanism and its application to the empirical realities of modern political community. The distinction I am making between the 'new cosmopolitanism' and 'cosmopolitan social theory' is analytical rather than substantive. Most of us who work in this area doubtless fall somewhere in between.

7   In its external manifestation, cosmopolitanism is a social form of right. It is realised in particular institutions, laws, norms and practices. If we conceive of modernity as a system of rights, then cosmopolitanism refers to the emergence of new forms of right in the sphere of inter-societal relations. These include international laws, international organisations such as the UN, international courts, global forms of governance, the idea of human rights, declarations and conventions on human rights, and mechanisms for securing peace between nations.

8   Cosmopolitan right presupposes a complex network of already existing social forms of right: first, the idea of right itself and its division into property rights, civil rights and rights of political participation; second, the 'moral point of view' that declares that individuals have the right to judge for themselves and should look inward to determine what is right and wrong; third, family and private life in which rights of love and friendship are meant to take pride of place; fourth, the rights of civil society and its constituent elements – the market, the system of justice and civil and political associations; and, finally, the

rights of the nation-state and its constituent elements – the constitution, the sovereign, the executive, the legislature and the judiciary. Cosmopolitanism is predicated, logically but not always historically, on the prior emergence of these social forms of right. In some circumstances the order of historical sequence might be reversed and cosmopolitan rights might precede other forms of right.

9   The emergence of cosmopolitan right is *necessary* because of the conflicts which tear apart all preceding forms of right and it is *possible* because of developments in the sphere of inter-societal relations. The *contradictory* nature of all forms of right indicates that the emergence of cosmopolitan right should not be seen as the apex of modernity, the culmination of the idea of right as such, or as the synthetic moment within which all previous divisions and conflicts are resolved. Cosmopolitanism is one element among many and contains within itself all that is worrying about every other social form of right. The validity of cosmopolitan forms of right is relative to other forms of right, including those of the nation-state, and it is never absolute.

10 Once cosmopolitanism emerges as a determinate social form, it transforms that which precedes it. It impacts upon the deployment of civil and political rights, on the exercise of moral judgements, on the practices of love and friendship, on the organisation of civil society and on the formation of the nation-state. Social life can never be the same again.

11 In its broad sense the 'cosmopolitan condition' (Kant's phrase) refers to the reconfiguration of the whole system of right once cosmopolitan forms of right are consolidated and impact on the whole. Modern political community is a complex and conflicted architectonic. It comprises a web of interrelated social forms. Cosmopolitan forms of right belong to this larger totality. Cosmopolitan social theory acknowledges the accomplishments of political modernity in developing a universal conception of humanity and it looks to the growth of new social forms to sustain this conception of humanity.

12 Cosmopolitan social theory maintains that to protect the old rights under current conditions, it is vital to construct new guarantees of human rights, new forms of law, new fields of public life, new political entities, new international institutions,

new avenues of mobility and not least new ways of thinking and acting in the world. It makes no assumption either that cosmopolitan social forms *supersede* the nation-state or that they are reconcilable with *existing* forms of the nation-state. Cosmopolitan social theory is a transformative as well as analytical project.

13 Subjectively, cosmopolitanism is a form of consciousness that involves an understanding of the concept of cosmopolitanism and a capacity to deploy this concept in imaginative and reflective ways. The 'objective' and 'subjective' aspects of cosmopolitanism belong closely together. The concept is nothing without its uses. It is the social form in which human beings struggle for mutual recognition as equals in the context of our multiple differences. Cosmopolitan social theory reconciles itself to the equivocations of cosmopolitanism and its effort to construct a normative perspective compatible with modernity's global reach, enlightened heritage and emancipatory promise.

14 Since Kant first thought about the cosmopolitan condition and what it is to view modernity from a cosmopolitan point of view, the downside of cosmopolitanism has always been on the agenda. Not every critique of methodological or political nationalism is cosmopolitan. Kant referred to the dangers of a world state, that it might conceal the interests of a world power or present its particular interests as if they were the universal interests of humanity or that it might itself secure a monopoly over global power. Today, with the experience of totalitarianism behind us, we know that global movements can be distrustful of national parochialism, transgressive of national borders and destructive of national unities and still pose a far greater threat to the idea of right than that posed by nations. Indeed, they can treat broad swathes of the global population as superfluous to requirement. The shadow of totalitarianism hangs over every effort to develop cosmopolitan social theory.

15 The sociological tradition includes many attempts to apply cosmopolitan ideas to modern political conditions. In his study of *The Germans* Norbert Elias follows the lead offered by Max Weber in emphasising the social pacification over time of *intra-societal* conflicts through the exercise of self-discipline on the part of individuals and the monopolisation of

the means of violence on the part of the state. He argues that at the *inter-societal* level, however, sociology has little to say about the absence of self-discipline among nation-states and the absence of legitimate authority able to restrain states from acts of violence. Elias articulated this absence as a problem for sociology: 'There is no monopoly of force on the international level. On this level we are basically still living exactly as our forefathers did in the period of their so-called 'barbarism' (Elias 1997: 176–7). The normative vista advocated by Elias was to establish social institutions at the inter-societal level equivalent to those found at the intra-societal level – institutions that could instil the habit of self-discipline on the part of states and determine, if not monopolise, the legitimate use of violence at the international level. Elias recognised that the monopoly of physical force by the state can be a dangerous weapon in the hands of the wrong people. Following Weber, the solution he looked to at the intra-societal level was not to dissolve the state monopoly of physical force but establish a form of state and a coterie of political actors who would not abuse this power. Elias conceived the task at the inter-societal level analogously: to establish a form of international federation that would have the authority to determine the legitimate use of violence and instil self-discipline on the part of nation-states without abusing the powers granted to it.

16 In the preface to *The Origins of Totalitarianism* Hannah Arendt writes that

> Anti-Semitism, imperialism and totalitarianism have demonstrated that human dignity needs a new guarantee which can be found only in a new political principle, a new law on earth, whose validity this time must comprehend the whole of humanity, while its power must remain strictly limited, rooted in and controlled by newly defined territorial entities.
>
> (Arendt 1979: ix)

She argued that world government provides no solution for it had its own capacity for barbarism:

> It is quite conceivable . . . that one fine day a highly
> organized and mechanized humanity will conclude quite
> democratically . . . that for humanity as a whole it would be
> better to liquidate certain parts thereof.
>
> (Arendt 1979: 299)

Arendt seeks to demonstrate that 'Universality' in the modern
age can mean only the universality of rights, that is, the right of
all human beings to have rights and the establishment of political
conditions capable of supporting the universality of rights: 'the
right to have rights, or the right of every individual to belong
to humanity, should be guaranteed by humanity itself' (Arendt
1979: 298).

17 The downfall of the right to have rights was not in the past
external to our civilisation and it remains an immanent
possibility for the future. The narrative of downfall is closely
tied to the history of the nation-state. The break-up of empires
after the First World War was accompanied by the rise of
nationalist movements proclaiming the right of nations to self-
determination. The principle of national self-determination,
advanced by nationalist movements and representatives of the
Great Powers was a principle of freedom, but it inverted the
relation between state and nation. It proclaimed that the nation
defines the state, the state does not define the nation. Since
there was practically no territory that did not contain a mix of
different peoples, this principle created its own exclusions:

> If in a mixed area one group makes good a territorial claim and
> establishes a nation-state, other groups will feel threatened
> and resentful. For them to be ruled by one group claiming to
> rule in its own national territory is worse than to be governed
> by an empire which does not base its title to rule on national
> grounds.
>
> (Kedourie 1993)

Many of those who lived together, albeit unequally, in the old
empires now found themselves belonging to conflicting nation-
states. Many were treated as minorities or second-class citizens
within these newly defined states. Many were expelled because

they did not belong to the nation-state. Many were displaced and deprived of the political community that might grant them the right to have rights. It was but a short step to ascribe their lack of rights to their own natural deficiencies. Totalitarian movements exploited the plight of 'pariah' peoples (today's undocumented migrants and asylum seekers) to characterise those deprived of rights as unworthy or incapable of possessing rights: 'If the world is not yet convinced that the Jews are the scum of the earth', Hitler wrote, 'it soon will be when unidentifiable beggars, without nationality, without money and without passports cross their frontiers' (Arendt 1979: 269). Once the right to have rights was repudiated for pariah people, it was but another short step to repudiate the idea of right itself. In this context the idea of the rights of man became the marker of what Giorgio Agamben calls 'naked man': one who has lost everything – country, home and place in the world (Agamben 1998).

18 The point of cosmopolitan social theory is to resist not to endorse the results of this process. Cosmopolitan social theory is an attempt to face up to and resist the transforming violence of the modern age. It does so not so much in the name of 'human right', which is today a particular sub-category of rights in general, but in the name of the right of every human being to have rights.

19 Cosmopolitan social theory is not a fashion due to be abandoned as new fashions enter the academic, intellectual or political marketplace. If the new cosmopolitanism makes the inflated claim that humanity is entering a period of universal human rights, perpetual peace and global governance, this is quickly matched by a reactive disillusionment which holds that nothing has changed, the world is an ever more dangerous place, we are subject to a new imperialism, and self-interest, bigotry, contingency and violence continue to be the true motor of human history. Cosmopolitan social theory is the enemy of the politics of disillusionment. Cosmopolitan social theory recognises that human history often looks more like a 'slaughter-bench' (Hegel's term) than a universal history reaching towards a cosmopolitan end. However, this indicates only that cosmopolitanism is no simple topic but a complex and

difficult phenomenon that taxes the resources of social theory. It creates as many clouds as it clears.

20 Cosmopolitan social theory understands social relations through a universalistic conception of humanity and by means of universalistic analytical tools and methodological procedures. Its simple but by no means trivial claim is that, despite all our differences, humankind is effectively one and must be understood as such.

21 This book is as much an exercise in cosmopolitan social theorising as it is a discussion of cosmopolitanism itself.

Acknowledgements

This book is the latest issue of some ten years' writing in the area of cosmopolitanism and social theory. In the course of this time I have had many people to thank for exchanging ideas, putting me right when I was wrong, having faith in my work and keeping me going in this area when other attractions were on offer. I want to acknowledge in particular two of my former doctoral students who have rapidly become independent and internationally renowned scholars in their own right: Dr Daniel Chernilo, Associate Professor in the Department of Sociology, Universidad Alberto Hurtado, Chile, and Dr William Smith, Lecturer in the Department of Politics, University of Dundee. I owe a particular debt to Dr Chernilo for his work on cosmopolitanism and the history of social theory and to Dr Smith for his work on the normative implications of cosmopolitan social theory. You will see from the bibliography that this book has a debt to the joint work I have done with both these colleagues. I have received extraordinarily helpful comments, warnings and encouragement from Vivienne Boon, Philosophy, Liverpool; Professor Robin Cohen, Sociology, Warwick; Dr Glynis Cousin, Higher Education Academy; Professor Gerard Delanty, Sociology, Sussex; Alison Diduck, Law, UCL; Professor Alessandro Ferrara, Philosophy, Rome; Dr David Hirsh, Sociology, Goldsmiths; Professor Maria Pia Lara, Philosophy, University Autonóma Metropolitana, Mexico; Professor Lydia Morris Sociology, Essex; Professor Alan Norrie, Law, King's London; Professor Istvan Pogany, Law, Warwick; Dr David Seymour, Law, Lancaster; Dr Charles Turner, Sociology, Warwick; Dr Rolando Vazquez, Sociology, Gothenburg; and Lawrence Welch, NHS, Bradford. My thanks too to the ESRC New Securities Programme for funding my project on 'Cosmopolitanism and military intervention: the elaboration of a paradigm' and to the organisers of the Annual Symposium on Philosophy and Social Science, Prague, for providing a particularly genial as well as productive forum for presenting ideas.

1

TAKING THE 'ISM' OUT OF COSMOPOLITANISM

Laying out the field

The physical dismantling of the Berlin Wall in 1989 offers a compelling image of the breaking down of boundaries maintained by force and of the re-opening of suppressed forms of human contact. This event appropriately marked the emergence of a new intellectual and political movement that is itself international and places human rights, international law, global governance and peaceful relations between states at the centre of its vision of the world. When we speak today of the 'new cosmopolitanism' it is this movement that we have in mind.

Within the social sciences cosmopolitanism has evolved since 1989 into a vibrant, interdisciplinary movement with its own distinctive research agenda (for edited collections see, for example, Archibugi 2004a; Archibugi *et al*. 1998; Beck and Sznaider 2006; Boon and Fine 2007; Breckenridge and Pollock 2002; Cheah and Robbins 1998; Held and McGrew 2002; Vertovec and Cohen 2003). The contours of this movement are not always well defined and it is traversed internally by all kinds of fault lines; and yet the new cosmopolitanism is an identifiable current gravitating around a number of shared commitments. These include: (a) the overcoming of national presuppositions and prejudices within the social scientific disciplines themselves and the reconstruction in this light of the core concepts we employ; (b) the recognition that humanity has entered an era of mutual interdependence on a world scale and the conviction that this worldly existence is not adequately understood within the terms of conventional social science; and (c) the development of normative and frankly prescriptive theories of world citizenship, global justice and cosmopolitan democracy. The dividing lines between these differentiated conceptual, societal and normative concerns are by no means always clear and it is possible to accept one without the other. All the social scientific disciplines have their own particular story to tell, though one of the strengths of the new cosmopolitanism from the start has been that it is an interdisciplinary project and that all its intradisciplinary stories are the products of considerable exchange across the disciplines.

THE NEW COSMOPOLITANISM WITHIN THE SOCIAL SCIENCES

In the field of international law cosmopolitanism displays a logic that extends the scope of the discipline and to some extent transcends its origins. International law is conventionally conceived as a form of law which recognises the individual nation-state as its unit of analysis and advances national self-determination and non-interference in the internal affairs of other states as its guiding principles. It imagines a world of sovereign freedom constrained by few international rules to constrain the behaviour of governments towards other states and towards their own citizens and subjects. Cosmopolitanism seeks to extend the reach of international law beyond issues of state sovereignty. It concerns itself with the rights and responsibilities of world citizens. One of the key problems it addresses is that some of the worst violators of human rights can be states or state-like formations. Whilst international law has traditionally developed according to the principle that every state is sovereign within its own territory, cosmopolitanism endorses legal limitations on how rulers may behave towards the ruled; and whilst international law leaves it to states to protect the rights of individuals, cosmopolitanism looks also to the formation of international legal bodies above the level of nation-states to perform this function. To be sure, there is a substantial grey area between state-centred and cosmopolitan conceptions of international law, but the core analytical distinction is between the conventional form of international law that recognises only states as legal subjects and limits the role of international bodies to that of protecting the sovereign rights of states and the cosmopolitan form of international law that extends its reach to the rights of individuals and freedoms of civil society associations on the one hand and to the widening legal authority of international bodies on the other (Archibugi 1995; Douglas 2001; Eleftheriadis 2003; Falk 1998, 1999; Hirsh 2003; Robertson 2006; Sands 2003, 2006).

In the field of international relations cosmopolitanism also contains a logic that extends the scope and transcends the origins of the discipline. The 'realist' mainstream of international relations holds that the state is the ultimate source of authority and by implication that there is no legal or moral authority beyond the plurality of sovereign states. In mainstream international relations the idea of an international system composed of independent and sovereign states, called 'Westphalian' after its origins in the Treaty of Westphalia of 1648, provides its normal point of departure. In realist international relations this 'anarchic' system of sovereign states is regarded as a natural and immutable order, a given for all analytical purposes, or in more historically informed accounts as a rational outcome of modernisation processes finally achieved at the end of history. The new cosmopolitanism criticises realism for its readiness to rationalise a system of sovereign states that is in fact historically specific and normatively conditional. It emphasises that the sovereignty of the state is itself a product of history rather than a permanent feature of the human condition and that its origins are to be explained rather than its ontological status assumed. It entertains the thought, excluded by realism, that the Westphalian system of sovereign states is in fact being surpassed. It breaks down the categorical distinction it sees in realism between the *domestic* field, in which individuals freely submit to the state as to their own rational will, and the *international* field, taken to be devoid of all ethical values. It rejects the temporal matrix which declares that *inside* the state progress can be accomplished over time but that *outside* there can be only an eternal repetition of power and interest. And it repudiates the intellectual rationalisation of a political order based on a lack of moral and legal inhibition as to how states relate to one another and especially as to how they relate to their own citizens and subjects. Its basic intuition is that many of the assumptions of the Westphalian model are still operative in international relations today but that the conditions for the reconstruction of international relations along cosmopolitan lines are now ripe (Bartelson 2001; Brown 2006; Doyle 1993; Held 1995a; Linklater 1998).

In the field of political philosophy the new cosmopolitanism is usually based on the revival of ideas of universal history, perpetual peace and cosmopolitan justice developed in the eighteenth century and formalised by Kant around the time of the French Revolution. The core contention is that the cosmopolitan ideals of Enlightenment thought are once again pertinent to our own times. The new cosmopolitanism sets itself the task of ironing out inconsistencies in Kant's way of thinking, radicalising it where its break from the old order of sovereign states was incomplete, freeing it from the old metaphysical baggage, elaborating linkages between peace and *social* justice which Kant neglected, and applying it to a radically transformed social context. The basic agenda of cosmopolitan political philosophy is to 'think with Kant against Kant' in reconstructing the cosmopolitan ideal for our own times. A crucial aspect of this programme is to reassess the normative value of nationalism. While advocates of the new cosmopolitanism are prepared to acknowledge that nationalism may have had value in the past, not least in the pursuit of anti-colonial struggles or in the building of modern welfare states, they renounce the idea that solidarity ties must be conceptually linked to the nation-state and pronounce the death of nationalism as a normative principle of social integration. The credo of the new cosmopolitanism is that the universalistic character of the idea of right, once swamped by the self-assertion of one nation against another, is best suited to the identity of *world citizens* and not to that of citizens of one state against another (Apel 1997; Archibugi 1995; Cavallar 1999; Fine 2001a, 2003a; Habermas 1998, 2001; Hoffe 2006; Kant 1991; Kuper 2000; Lara and Fine 2007; Nussbaum 2002; O'Neill 2000; Pogge 2001; Rawls 1999; Smith and Fine 2004).

My final example is in the field of sociology and social theory. Here the rise of cosmopolitan thinking is closely aligned with attempts to dissociate the core concepts of social theory, especially that of 'society' itself, from the presuppositions of the nation-state. It is argued that a strong notion of *national* society has prevailed within the sociological tradition as a result both of the discipline's own nationalistic consciousness and of the actual solidity and expansion of national societies during the time of sociology's development. The new cosmopolitanism maintains that the concept of 'society' was shaped at birth by a coincidence between the rise of sociology as a discipline and the formation of nation-states as *the* modern form of political community. It emphasises the historicity of this conceptual framework and its inappropriateness for understanding social life in an age of globalisation. Its conviction is that the old national framework of sociological analysis is no longer capable of dealing with the major social transformations currently taking place under the register of globalisation: the proliferation of connections between societies, the growth of power structures outside national frameworks of accountability; the proliferation of global risks (of an ecological, political, economic, epidemic, criminal and terrorist character) that have no respect for national boundaries; the increasing movement of people across national frontiers and the resulting heterogeneity of populations in most modern societies; growing numbers of undocumented migrants and asylum seekers; and the increasing importance of international political and regulatory bodies. The new cosmopolitanism holds that such changes in social life indicate the need for a corresponding change in social theory – one which takes the world and not the nation-state as its primary unit of analysis. Its project is to free social theory from a world that no longer exists and overcome those categories of understanding and standards of judgement which depend on a moribund national framework (Albrow 1996; Beck 2006a; Castells 2000; Delanty 2000; Urry 2000).

This brief outline of the parameters of the new cosmopolitanism is anything but exhaustive; it is intended only to illustrate the parameters of the new cosmopolitanism within the social sciences and how the new cosmopolitanism presents itself in this context. At the core of the cosmopolitan project is the notion that social science has in the past made its peace with the nation-state and the conviction that this reconciliation with reality must now be overcome. The new cosmopolitanism is an endeavour to denature and decentre the nation-state – to loosen the ties that bind the nation-state to theories of democracy in political theory, theories of society in sociology, theories of internationalism in international relations, theories of sovereignty in international law and theories of justice in political philosophy. We should add theories of culture in cultural studies and theories of space in human geography. Its critical function is to emancipate social science from its bounded national presuppositions and construct new analytical concepts appropriate to globalising times. My question, however, is whether the new cosmopolitanism is as new or as cosmopolitan as it suggests. To explore this issue further, I am now going to narrow my focus and concentrate for a moment on the work of one sociologist who has arguably done more than any other to construct the new cosmopolitanism over the last decade: Ulrich Beck.

ULRICH BECK AND THE CRITIQUE OF METHODOLOGICAL NATIONALISM

In a path-breaking series of essays and books spanning the last decade (1998a, 2000a, 2000b, 2002a, 2002b, 2003, 2006a, 2006b, 2007) Beck has campaigned persistently and urgently for the overcoming of the tradition of 'methodological nationalism' within sociology and for the development of a 'methodological cosmopolitanism' in its place. I want to address here one aspect of his multifaceted work: the time-consciousness, that is, the conception of past, present and future, which informs his cosmopolitan vision. The rigidities of how he conceives the relation between past and future may serve as an exemplar of a wider problem within the new cosmopolitanism – and one that rightly worries the most astute observers (Chernilo 2007a,b, 2008a).

Beck argues that traditional sociology has equated the idea of 'society' with the nation-state and that it has simply assumed that humanity is naturally divided into a limited number of nations: 'It is a nation-state outlook', Beck writes, 'that governs the sociological imagination' (Beck 2002b: 51). He maintains that the solidity and self-sufficiency of the nation-state are now being shattered and that this social transformation places upon sociology the responsibility to re-invent itself as 'a transnational science ... released from the fetters of methodological nationalism' (Beck 2002b: 53–4). He writes of the 'obsolescence' of traditional social theories and their 'zombie categories' and looks to the emancipation of social theory from the old 'container theory of society'. Beck sees the canon and tradition of social theory dominated by the conceptualisations of methodological nationalism: 'The possibility that the unity of state and nation might dissolve, disintegrate or undergo a complete trans-formation remains beyond the purview of the social sciences' (Beck 2006a: 29). He stands for the replacement of the old 'methodological nationalism', which used to dominate the social sciences, with a new 'methodological cosmopolitanism' that is capable of tackling 'what had previously been analytically excluded' (Beck 2002b: 52). Beck concedes we can find partial arguments in the history of sociology that point beyond methodological nationalism, but is insistent that there has been no serious questioning within sociology of the unity of state and nation until the emergence of the new cosmopolitanism itself.

The critique of 'methodological nationalism' actually goes back to the 1970s when a number of sociologists, including Anthony Giddens (1973) and Herminio Martins (1974), argued that a major defect of existing social science was the treatment of nation-states *as if* they were closed, autonomous and self-contained units. Their contention was that the limited vision of methodological national-ism led to predominantly endogenous explanations of social change and that this explanatory bias had to be rectified (Smelser 1997; Wagner 1994). Beck radicalised this critique of prevailing sociologi-cal theories of social change and turned it into a far more general dis-satisfaction with the sociological tradition (Chernilo 2006a, 2006b, 2007a). He presents the critique of methodological nationalism not so much as a contribution *within* the tradition of social theory but as a major rupture in the history of social theory – one made neces-sary by the era of radical epochal change in which we now live.

Now, a sense of rupture, of epochal change is widely shared within social theory. It is evident, for instance, in the classification of modernity into 'periods': modernity and postmodernity, high modernity and late modernity, first modernity and second moder-nity, solid modernity and liquid modernity, national modernity and postnational modernity. It is a vital part of social theory to identify what is new in social and political life and to think about what this entails for social and political thought. We cannot assume that old concepts suffice to convey new phenomena. For example, it can be positively misleading to assume that concepts of power drawn from a pre-totalitarian age will be sufficient to understand the unprecedented forms of terror and annihilation brought into existence by totalitarian movements. We must always question whether the words we use have caught up with our experiences.

However, the sense of epochal change that plays so large a role in social theory can itself be misleading if it simply makes a cult out of novelty. We live in an age in which 'the new' is proclaimed from every advertising banner and contemporary social theory is itself a creature of our age. It too is inclined to speak freely of *new* forms of democracy, *new* forms of war, *new* types of personal relationship and so forth. Too often however, it does so on the basis of homogenised views of the past and without consideration of the multiple ways in which the past weighs upon the present. We cannot simply set aside concepts, like old hats we remove from our heads, without considering whence they came and what work they do (Young-Bruehl 2006). New concepts have to be squared with new realities or they too can become a constraint on our thinking. Today there is nothing new in declaring the new, and the claim that this or that event is 'unprecedented' and that there are no words to describe it has itself become almost a commonplace of philosophical discourse (Habermas and Derrida 2003a).

The cult of the new, if we may call it thus, can be illustrated through Beck's analysis of the destruction of the World Trade Center. 9/11, he writes, stands for the 'complete collapse of language'. It signals the bankruptcy of all national frames of reference. It indicates the 'global community of fate' to which we are all now bound. It demonstrates that in a world risk society we need a 'new big idea', that of cosmopolitanism itself (Beck 2002a: 48). Beck likens the advent of cosmopolitan norms in our own times to the sea-change achieved by the Peace of Westphalia in the seventeenth century. He declares that it marks the advent of a 'second Enlightenment' – one that will 'open our eyes and our institutions to the immaturity of the first industrial civilization and the dangers it posed to itself' (Beck 2002b: 50). He argues that 9/11 confronts the world with an existential choice: not only between nationalism and multilateralism but also between regressive multilateralism based on surveillance states and progressive multilateralism based on cosmopolitan states. A multilateralism based on surveillance states sacrifices rights, law, democracy and hospitality to the security of the Western citadel. A multilateralism based on cosmopolitan principles also seeks security but by means of human rights, international law, democracy and hospitality at the transnational level. 9/11, he writes, brings to the surface the defining characteristic of our age – that risks are now spatially de-territorialised and uncontrollable at the level of the nation-state and that it is necessary to construct a new principle of cosmopolitan order transcending both the classical framework of nation-states and the imposition of police powers at the international level.

Over against the cult of the new, I do not wish to suggest that there is *nothing* new in the kind of terrorism practised on 9/11. On the contrary, it seems to me that recent attempts to analogise this event to the *old* totalitarianism of Stalin and Hitler or to the *old* uses of terror in national liberation movements are equally inadequate ways of dealing with what is new in this case. But to speak of a 'complete collapse of language' diminishes our ability to *understand* the event. No understanding is possible without analytical concepts against which to measure what is new. While all social theory tries to make sense of a rapidly transforming world, the idea of crisis only makes sense against a backdrop which allows us to see what has changed (Habermas 1988).

THE CRITIQUE OF THE CRITIQUE OF METHODOLOGICAL NATIONALISM

The other side of the coin of being stuck in old ways of thinking is what Frank Webster has termed the 'fallacy of presentism' (Webster 2002: 267). The fallacy of presentism refers to the tendency to turn the present into an 'ism' and *prematurely* declare the redundancy of old concepts and theories. The paradox of 'presentism' may be illustrated by the observation that while Beck argues in relation to 9/11 for the need for *new* categories of understanding and *new* standards of judgement to deal with this event, he declares his own debt to the seventeenth-century political philosophy of Thomas Hobbes and poses his analysis of global risk society in Hobbesian terms (Beck 2002a: 46) concerning the risks that arise in global society and the conditions of achieving security in these circumstances.

Beck's representation of the history of the nation-state strangely mirrors the 'methodological nationalism' he criticises. He argues that 'national organization as a structuring principle of societal and political action can *no longer* serve as a premise for the social science observer perspective' (Beck 2002b: 52, my italic), implying that in the past this national principle may well have been an appropriate premise. According to this account, methodological nationalism was right for its own times, though obsolete for ours, and Beck criticises it only from a historical point of view (Joas 2003). The fairly obvious point to make is that a methodologically nationalist social science has *never* been able to provide a satisfactory account of nation-states even during the 'first age of modernity' (Chernilo 2006a). If this is so, then Beck is to be faulted not for criticising methodological nationalism but rather for accepting too readily its historical validity. 'Methodological nationalism' is an approach that naturalises or rationalises the existence of the nation-state. It locates the development of the nation-state in a teleological framework as the apex of modern political community. It imposes the concept of the nation-state upon all political formations which have emerged or survived in the modern period, including multinational empires, totalitarian regimes, east and west power blocs, city states and transnational bodies such as the European Union. It treats the nation-state as *the* characteristic form of political community of the modern age, or at least of the first modernity, and presumes its solidity, centrality and increasing pervasiveness. The problem with the critique of methodological nationalism, as Beck formulates it, is that it accepts the premises of methodological nationalism and differs only in declaring the advent of a new epoch, a second modernity, in which the national principle of political organisation finally gives way to the cosmopolitan.

Analogous issues arise in relation to international relations, where Beck writes of the changing grammar of the term 'international' and the hollowing of the 'fetish concepts' of state and nation (Beck 2006a: 37). He represents the 'Westphalian' order of independent nation-states as the framework of international relations in the 'first modernity' and characterises it as a Hobbesian state of nature writ large, a perpetual war of all states against all, in which no state could be secure. However, he also represents this anarchic model as remarkably stable – enduring for over 300 years from the Peace of Westphalia of 1648 right up to our own times. He acknowledges that the Westphalian order has assumed different shapes and forms in the course of its progressive evolution but his basic contention is that no fundamental change to the system of nation-states occurred before the transition to the new cosmopolitan epoch. Events as momentous as eighteenth-century political revolutions, the growth of imperialism in the nineteenth century, the collapse of mainland empires after the First World War, the formation of a raft of newly independent nation-states out of their fragments, the rise of totalitarian regimes with anti-national and global ambitions in the inter-war period, the collapse of overseas empires after the Second World War, a further raft of newly independent ex-colonial states, and the formation of two 'camps' during the Cold War – all such events are presented as punctuation marks in a continuous and expanding Westphalian narrative. Even the forms of international co-operation established among nation-states, such as the formation of the United Nations, and the emergence of a world system of independent nation-states appear merely to consolidate the fundamental principle of national sovereignty (Giddens 1985).

In this representation of history all events prior to the rise of the new cosmopolitan order seem only to consolidate and generalise the 'old' order of independent nation-states, as if the hoary chestnut, *le plus ça change, le plus c'est la même chose*, held absolute sway in the sphere of life. The 'new' cosmopolitan order appears as a product of our own age and not least of the work of the new cosmopolitans themselves. This teleological reconstruction of the history of the nation-state in the past allows for a spectacular image of the radical disjuncture occurring in the present. And yet the dependence of methodological cosmopolitanism on the methodological nationalism it seeks to overcome becomes all the more pronounced. Both conceive of a rupture between tradition and modernity in the mid-seventeenth century marked by the Treaty of Westphalia. Both conceive of the nation-state as the governing principle of modern political community. Methodological cosmopolitanism differs from methodological nationalism only in that it refuses to see the nation-state as an end of history and proposes a second rupture, one which brings into being the cosmopolitan condition (Wagner 2001: 83).[1]

I am arguing that Beck concedes too much to methodological nationalism when he intimates that it did *once* have a historical validity. I would also suggest that the critique of methodological nationalism has in fact been a fairly constant feature of social theory, even if it is executed in uneven and inconsistent ways (Chernilo 2007a,b; Turner 2006). For example, Emile Durkheim's appeal to the cosmopolitan moral foundations of the modern state was more explicit than most. He looked to the reconciliation of cosmopolitanism and patriotism by shifting the priorities of national rivalry from war to peaceable competition. He wrote:

> If each State had as its chief aim not to expand or to lengthen its borders, but to set its own house in order and to make the widest appeal to its members for a moral life on an ever higher level, then all discrepancy between national and human morals would be excluded . . . The more societies concentrate their energies inwards, on the interior life, the more they will be diverted from the disputes that bring a clash between cosmopolitanism – or world patriotism, and patriotism . . . Societies can have their pride, not in being the greatest or the wealthiest, but in being the most just, the best organised and in possessing the best moral constitution.

(Durkheim 1992: 74–5)[2]

In the case of Marx, we find not only a normative commitment to 'internationalism' rather than nationalism but more significantly an analysis of the erosion of national boundaries by global capitalism and a critique of the dynamics of capital accumulation in which national characteristics play a strictly subordinate part. Weber for his part objected to any treatment of nations as 'individuals' or 'biological entities', indeed to any hypostatisation of the nation as a 'social-psychological unity which experiences development in itself', and he rejected attempts to understand social life through notions of 'common blood', 'shared culture' or '*Volkgeist*' (Chernilo 2007b: 29–30). It is interesting to note that contemporary German critics of his *Science as a Vocation* (1919) objected to the non-nationalistic worldview and 'un-German' universalism that ran through the text (Schluchter 1996: 39–45). Similarly, Simmel advanced a universal conception of society as a sphere of 'reciprocal influencing' and warned against any treatment of society as a 'collective name'. The universalism of sociological conceptions of society is a question that deserves a book on its own (Chernilo 2007a).

I do not suggest that these critiques of methodological national-ism were necessarliy successful. For instance, Durkheim's fusion of *la patrie* and cosmopolitanism proved no obstacle to the expression of vehemently anti-German sentiments during the First World War, based on a critique of the militaristic and anti-Semitic nationalism of one German, Heinrich von Treitschke. I suggest only that the approach of sociology to the science of the social contains within it an opposition to methodological nationalism. Classical sociology saw itself not as a repudiation of enlightenment universalism but as its empirical manifestation (Wagner 2006).The key point is certainly not to defend the sociological tradition *tout court* against the charge of methodological nationalism but to consider why this charge has been so stressed and over-extended within the new cosmopolitan-ism.[3] For in both 'old' social theory and the 'new' cosmopolitanism we are confronted with the difficult question of the positioning of the nation-state in the context of the global reshaping of modernity.

The temporal frame of Beck's critique of methodological nation-alism lends itself to a particularly negative view of the sociological tradition. He presents 'humanistic universalism' as the key charac-teristic of Enlightenment thought and describes it as a universal-ism that tends towards greater sameness and the elimination of plurality.

> Universalism obliges us to respect others as equals in principle, yet for that very reason does not involve any requirement that would inspire curiosity or respect for what makes other differ-ent . . . the particularity of others is sacrificed to an assumed universal equality which denies its own origins and interests. Universalism becomes thereby two-faced: respect and hegem-ony, rationality and terror.
>
> (Beck 2006a:49)

Beck argues that the humanistic universalism of Enlightenment thought gave way to the methodological nationalism of social theory, which elevated its national conception of society over and above any universal conception of humanity. He finally presents cosmopolitanism as the reconciliation of the universalism of the Enlightenment and the methodological nationalism of the social sciences: on the one hand, it presupposes a 'universalistic minimum' to be upheld at all costs and 'universal procedural norms' to regulate the cross-cultural treatment of difference; on the other, it 'does not negate nationalism but presupposes it and transforms it into cosmopolitan nationalism' (Beck 2006a: 49). The cosmopolitan vision, according to Beck, permits people to 'view themselves simultaneously as part of a threatened world and as part of their local situation and histories'. It indicates 'recognition of difference beyond the misunderstandings of territoriality and homogenisation' (Beck 2006a: 30). It replaces the 'either–or' mentality of the past, be it the humanistic universalism of the Enlightenment or the methodological nationalism of social theory, with the 'both–and' consciousness of the evolving cosmopolitan future. (An alternative way of putting this might be that the new cosmopolitanism presents itself as the *synthesis* of an old-fashioned modernist humanism on the one side and postmodern identity politics on the other.[4])

Beck wishes to construct cosmopolitanism in a way that is incompatible with all homogenising claims. His aim is not to advance cosmopolitanism as an abstraction ruling over the plurality of particular national needs and interests nor as a power to which nations must bow as if to their own rational will, but as the rational form in which the universal and the particular are finally reconciled. This kind of synthesis sometimes goes under the name of 'post-universalism'. I would argue, however, that this cosmopolitanism vision is not as radical or new as it seems and that its equivocations go to the heart of political modernity (Löwith 1967).

POST-UNIVERSALISM AND THE MODERN STATE

The term 'cosmopolitanism' goes back to antiquity and its ancient connotations still have resonance among modern writers (Fine and Cohen 2003; Nussbaum 1991). Martha Nussbaum defines the cosmopolitan as one whose politics is 'based upon reason rather than patriotism or group sentiment' and is 'truly universal *rather* than communitarian' (Nussbaum 1997). Nussbaum looks to antiquity not only as the origin but as the inspiration of cosmopolitanism. She looks back to Zeno's 'cosmopolis' – a world-city based on a common law for all humanity in which even barbarians and slaves could be citizens; to Diogenes's dissenting claim to be a 'citizen of the world', a claim denounced by Plutarch as absurd as well as dangerous; to Cicero's faith in a 'society of humanity' and the 'common right of humanity'; and to Seneca's maxim that 'we look neither to this corner nor to that, but measure the boundaries of our nation by the sun'. While the ancient cosmopolitan tradition was not 'innocent', based either on the elevation of the Greek *polis* as a model for the world or on the ambition of the Roman Empire to turn the world into a common people under its own rule (Pagden 2000), it still embodied an emphatic idea of universality and an equally emphatic repudiation of patriotism and other group loyalties.

What makes modern cosmopolitanism *modern*, however, is not so much that it stands for a universal human community over and above local loyalties, but rather that it seeks to *reconcile* the idea of universal species-wide human solidarity with particular solidarities that are smaller and more specific than the human species (Hollinger 2001: 238). This reconciliation takes many forms. For example, John Stuart Mill insisted that the principle of *patriotisme éclairé* he proposed, which he distinguished from 'nationality in the vulgar sense of the term; a senseless antipathy to foreigners', was compatible with 'the general welfare of the human race' and he wrote of the capacity of human beings, properly educated, to attain an 'ideal devotion' not only to their own country but to 'a greater country, the world':

> When we consider how ardent a sentiment, in favourable circumstances, of education, *the love of country* has become, we cannot judge it impossible that *the love of that larger country, the world*, may be nursed into similar strength.
>
> (Mill, *System of Logic*, cited in Varouxakis 2006: 101–2)

We have already noted that Emile Durkheim looked to the reconciliation of cosmopolitanism and patriotism through shifting the priorities of national rivalry from war to peaceable competition.

The 'new cosmopolitanism' follows closely in these 'modernist' footsteps. Kwame Anthony Appiah (1996) appeals to the concept of 'cosmopolitan patriotism' to convey the idea that a sense of belonging to a particular community is a necessary aspect of turning cosmopolitanism into a desirable and realisable political project. Jürgen Habermas looks to the reconciliation of cosmopolitan values, laws and institutions with the re-affirmation of national and transnational identity in the form of 'constitutional patriotism' (2001: 74–6). Will Kymlicka (1995) warns of the danger of constitutional patriotism being used by existing nation-states to crush minority rights and seeks to construct a cosmopolitanism that will also protect national minorities. Ulrich Beck, as we have seen, argues that cosmopolitanism, far from negating nationalism, 'presupposes it and transforms it into cosmopolitan nationalism' (Beck 2006a: 49). The concept of 'cosmopolitan nationalism' may sound rather like kosher bacon, but Beck is not alone in insisting that the stabilising and integrative factors enlightened patriotism provides are required by cosmopolitanism. In short, the new cosmopolitanism draws its appeal from the contrast between ancient and modern conceptions of political community: the former aspiring for a universal in which the rights of particular solidarities remain downplayed or invalidated; the latter aspiring for a universalistic world compatible with the rights of particular solidarities (Hollinger 2001).[5]

The strength of the ancient conception of cosmopolitanism lies in its critical purchase: it offers a clear-cut critique of nationalism, patriotism and other 'local' manifestations of political modernity. The strength of the modern conception of cosmopolitanism lies in its embrace of the core principle of political modernity, the integration of particular rights of subjective freedom with the common good. The question arises, however, as to the *critical* purchase of the modern conception: how far does it offer a critique of political modernity or an adaptation to it. The new cosmopolitanism can sometimes appear as immensely radical and transformative and at other times as little more than a gloss on the existing political order.

When the new cosmopolitanism appeals to 'post-universalism', to what Beck terms a 'both–and' rather than an 'either–or' consciousness, this appeal forgets that the awesome power of the modern state derives from its already being 'both–and' from the start. Let me cite Hegel in support of this claim. In his own peculiar style he writes in *The Philosophy of Right*:

> The principle of modern states has enormous strength and depth because it allows the principle of subjectivity to attain fulfilment in the *self-sufficient extreme* of personal particularity, while at the same time *bringing it back to substantial unity* and

> so preserving this unity in the principle of subjectivity itself.
> The essence of the modern state is that the universal should be
> linked with the complete freedom of particularity and the well-
> being of individuals . . . the universality of the end cannot make
> further progress without the personal knowledge and volition of
> particular individuals who must retain their rights . . . the univer-
> sal must be activated, but subjectivity on the other hand must
> be developed as a living whole. Only when both moments are
> present in full measure can the state be regarded as articulated
> and truly organised.
>
> (Hegel 1991, §124)

The principle of the modern state is that it represents both the
public interest and the particular interests of individuals within it.
What makes the modern state modern is that it allows the principle
of individuality to attain complete fulfilment whilst at the same time
bringing it back to the unity of the whole. What is this principle
but that of 'both–and'? Hegel argues that the conjunction of the
universal and the particular not only gives to the modern state a self-
consciously liberal aspect, as the locus of reconciliation between the
public interest and private rights, but also feeds the megalomania
of the modern state since what the state is and does appears as the
rational will of every individual within it. It evaporates the real
antagonisms between the individual and the state. It mystifies their
relation.[6] The 'both–and' quality of the modern state is an integral
part of its power. By treating its own will as the will of every individual, it feeds its most dangerous totalitarian fantasies.

In identifying cosmopolitanism with the both–and consciousness of post-universalism, the new cosmopolitanism engages not
so much with the critique of the modern state, the fetishism of its
power, as with transferring the logic of reconciliation to a higher
level.

THE COSMOPOLITAN VISION

The cosmopolitan vision, as Beck advances it, is more about the
future than the past. It is predominantly not about what the world
of nation-states was like but what the world is becoming and how
our consciousness is changing with it. For Beck, orientation to the

future sometimes appears as a cosmopolitan principle. He writes that in world risk society 'the past loses its power to determine the present. Instead, the future – something non-existent, constructed or fictitious – takes its place as the cause of present experience and action' (Beck 2000c: 100). He contrasts the 'future-oriented legitimacy' and 'visionary non-fiction' of cosmopolitan sociology with both the 'more-of-the-same dogma' of traditional sociology and teleological conceptions of historical progress, and hopes in this manner to comprehend a situation that is 'still to manifest its full development' (Beck 2000b: 8–9).

Beck insists there is a sense in which 'reality itself has become cosmopolitan' and refers to the emergence of what he calls, enticingly, a 'banal, everyday and forced cosmopolitanism' (Beck 2006a). The question is this: even if we are prepared to concede that cosmopolitanism is not only 'forced' but also contains its own propensities to the use of force, in what sense can we say that 'reality itself has become cosmopolitan'? On closer inspection the justification of this claim rests more on the development of a certain kind of consciousness than on any social transformation. For example, Beck refers to mass migration and the resulting growth of heterogeneous and hybrid populations in most modern societies in support of the proposition that reality has become cosmopolitan. He immediately concedes, however, that there is nothing new in this phenomenon and that what has changed is the emergence of a new kind of political and cultural awareness which affirms the mixing of peoples. He writes: 'From the very beginning the emerging global market required the mixing of peoples . . . What is new is not forced mixing but awareness of it, its self-conscious political affirmation' (Beck 2006a: 21). However, the self-conscious political affirmation of the mixing of peoples is unfortunately highly contested in the present day and co-exists with all manner of rival and reactive nationalisms. Similarly, when Beck refers to the explosion of global risks, he argues that these risks cannot be addressed by nation-states acting alone and create 'inescapable' pressures for states to co-operate across national boundaries. However, there is nothing new in the need for states to co-operate with other states and today, in the face of ecological and terrorist crises, the pressures on states to co-operate are proving anything but inescapable. As Beck well knows, there are many who argue that the West is divided over the question of whether to affirm

co-operation through international law or to take the road of hegemonic unilateralism and that ecological crises are as likely to lead to
new conflicts as to new forms of co-operation.

Is there a sense nonetheless in which we can say with Beck that
'reality has become cosmopolitan'? I think a reference to Kantian
natural law theory might help illuminate Beck's proposition. When
Kant referred to his own times as an 'age of enlightenment', he did
not mean to say that his age was enlightened but that enlightenment
was ethically the most defensible philosophical project of his age. In
What is Enlightenment? he formulated the issue thus:

> If it is now asked whether we at present live in an *enlightened* age,
> the answer is no, but we do live in an age of enlightenment. As
> things are at present, we still have a long way to go . . . But we
> do have distinct indications that the way is now being cleared
> for them to work freely in this direction . . . Men will of their own
> accord gradually work their way out of barbarism so long as arti-
> ficial measures are not deliberately adopted to keep them in it.
> (Kant 1991: 58)

If it is now asked *What is Cosmopolitanism?* the equivalent
answer might run along these lines. We do not live in a cosmopolitan
age but we do live in an age of cosmopolitanism. As things are, we
have a long way to go but we do have distinct indications that the
way is being cleared for a cosmopolitan future so long as artificial
measures are not deliberately adopted to prevent it. The age of cosmopolitanism may be understood more as a normative perspective
for viewing the potentialities and necessities of our age than as an
objective characterisation of the age itself. The cosmopolitan vision
may be understood in this context as spelling out the rational direction humankind would take so long as artificial measures are not
adopted to prevent this outcome. If the devil lies in the detail of this
qualification, it also reveals the natural law framework in which the
new cosmopolitanism continues to be posed.

COSMOPOLITANISM AND ITS CRITICS

The new cosmopolitanism meets with criticism from many sides
and my interest here is not to add to the list. On a factual level,

critics allude to the short-term or downright illusory character of cosmopolitan reforms: just as previous cosmopolitan initiatives were extinguished under the pressure of power politics, so too the cosmopolitan precedents established since 1989 may prove equally provisional (Zolo 1997, 1999). Alternatively, critics accept that the order of sovereign nation-states is being surpassed but provide a far more pessimistic reading of the post-national constellation that is replacing it. What is presented in the guise of cosmopolitanism may be revealed as the dominance of global capital over the life-world or of America over the globe. In this case cosmopolitanism is not criticised for the claim that the democratic structures and political life of the nation-state are becoming obsolete, but for its failure to see that this social transformation only intensifies the abstract character of domination. Hardt and Negri, for example, discern in the present the transformation of rival nations into a singular, overwhelming Empire, though they construct a kind of 'cosmopolitanism from below' in which an unbounded and nationally indistinct multitude is metamorphosed into the permanently resistant subject of global revolt (Hardt and Negri 2000).

Criticism is made of the cultural assumptions, national prejudices and power positions that remain intact behind the apparently universalistic discourse of the new cosmopolitanism, which leads critics to construe it as a mask for the imposition of 'Western' values on the 'East' and 'South', or as an instrument serving the political and financial interests of the sole remaining super-power. Critics argue that the cosmopolitan propensity to devalue state sovereignty coincides with the interests of American expansionism and is invoked only when American interests are at stake. Cosmopolitanism is charged with perpetuating the myth that the current global order is ruled by universal ideals and a supranational body authorised to enforce these ideals, whereas it is actually ruled by a hierarchy of co-operating and competing nation-states – different from the Westphalian order only in the fact that never before has one nation dominated others as the USA has done since 1989 (Chomsky 1999; Douzinas 2000). Some 'Schmittian' critics object to cosmopolitanism on the grounds not only that it expresses the hypocrisy of great powers but that it is used by great powers to moralise war and demonise their enemies (Agamben 2005).

Such criticisms are deeply destructive of the cosmopolitan enterprise and it is not difficult to discern the flaws in actually existing cosmopolitanism, which its critics are quick to exploit. It can be usurped by power. It can display the vanity of thinking that it has discovered a new 'Truth' on which the future of the globe depends and the innocence of thinking that the past no longer bears down on the present. It can perpetuate the myth of novelty and show contempt for ways of thinking it declares obsolete. It can assume the world has to be invented anew and it can be over-confident in its own prescriptions. If a distinguishing mark of nationalism is to get its own history wrong (Hobsbawm 1994), the same may be said of the new cosmopolitanism: it can paint the past grey on grey the better to declare its own futuristic brilliance. Such defects do exist, but this is no reason to abandon cosmopolitanism, only to reflect on its own shortcomings and to remedy them.

Criticism can fall short of what it criticises. Hegel once wrote that 'hatred of right is the shibboleth whereby fanaticism, imbecility and hypocritical good intentions manifestly . . . reveal themselves' (Hegel 1991 §258fn). I think this is true of hatred of the idea of cosmopolitan right. Even if cosmopolitanism becomes stuck at the level of conceptual thinking, it remains superior to a criticism that has no understanding of the concept and sees in world history nothing but power, self-interest and contingency. The ignominious history of twentieth-century hatred towards cosmopolitanism may be illustrated through the stigmatisation of the 'rootless cosmopolitan Jew'. Eleonore Koffman tells the story of how cultural conservatives (such as Carlyle, Spengler and Sombart) complained of the impure culture of 'cosmopolitan cities', notably Vienna, into which Jewish emancipation in the nineteenth century had brought an influx of Jewish immigrants. Jews were represented as a corrupting element, foreign to the nation, rootless and without homeland, the personification of the cosmopolitan (Koffman 2007; Traverso 1997). This way of thinking was inherited by a Stalinist political culture which abhorred uprootedness and treated cosmopolitanism as synonymous with betrayal of the motherland (Buck-Morss 2002). Mass arrests of Jewish intellectuals and repression of Jewish culture after the Second World War were perpetrated under the banner of campaigns against 'rootless cosmopolitans' as well as against 'Zionists'. Such stigmatisation of cosmopolitanism indicates to me only that there is something very valuable to preserve.

2

COSMOPOLITANISM AND NATURAL LAW
Kant and Hegel

I have suggested in the last chapter that the new cosmopolitanism has an affinity with natural law theory. This is indicated in its return to Kant and in particular its rediscovery and reconstruction of Kant's political essays on 'perpetual peace' and the 'cosmopolitan point of view' written over a 12-year period around the time of the French revolution (Kant 1991).[1] They are now widely regarded as the key philosophical origins of the new cosmopolitanism (Bohman and Lutz-Bachmann 1997). In this chapter I shall outline Kant's approach to cosmopolitanism and the natural law framework within which it is posed. My interest is in pursuing the question of the transition from natural law theory to cosmopolitan social theory and I shall argue that a crucial link-person in this transition, despite his reputation as philosopher of the state, is Hegel.

KANT'S THEORY OF COSMOPOLITANISM

Kant elaborated in his *Metaphysics of Justice* (Kant 1965) a detailed and systematic analysis of republicanism within the framework of the modern nation-state. He began with the analysis of private law, placing property rights within the realm of natural laws to which 'an obligation can be recognised *a priori* by reason without external legislation' (Kant 1965: 26). From this starting point he engaged in a series of 'deductions' from the postulates of practical reason: the idea of the 'person' as a possessor of rights whose 'moral personality is nothing but the freedom of a rational being under moral laws' (Kant 1965: 24); the idea of a 'thing' (*res*) as 'an object of free will that itself lacks freedom'; the separation of property from possession; the idea that there is nothing in the world which cannot be made into property, and so forth.

Kant then moved on to the sphere of public law. From the 'Idea of the state as it ought to be' Kant deduced the institutional forms of a republican constitution: a representative legislature to establish universal norms, an executive to subsume particular cases under these universal norms, a judiciary to determine what is right in cases of conflict, and the constitutional principle of the separation of powers to maintain these distinct spheres of activity in accordance with the 'moments of its concept' (Kant 1965: §45). Kant drew on social contract theory and moral philosophy to produce an image of a just state grounded in reason, the perfect *societat civilis* that would allow republican government to unfold even in a 'race of devils' (Ellis 2005: 36).

Having analysed private and public law within the framework of the nation-state, Kant turned his focus to the sphere of interstate or international law. He attacked what he called the 'depravity' of the existing 'Westphalian' order in which 'each state sees its own majesty ... precisely in not having to submit to any external legal constraint' and in which 'the glory of its ruler consists in his power to order thousands of people to immolate themselves for a cause which does not truly concern them, while he need not himself incur any danger whatsoever' (Kant 1991: 103). He criticised this model as one in which either there was no notion of international law or international law was interpreted merely as a right to go to war, which was in effect no law at all. He was critical of the legal architects of this model: traditional natural law theorists (Francisco Suarez 1548–1617, Hugo Grotius 1583–1645, Samuel Pufendorf 1632–94 and Emmerich von Vattel 1714–67), whom he lumped together as 'sorry comforters ... dutifully quoted in justification of military aggression'. He argued that they painted a thin legal gloss over a system in which sovereigns granted themselves the licence to use any means of warfare deemed necessary, exploit newly discovered colonies as if they were 'lands without owners', and treat foreigners as enemies without rights (Kant 1991: 105–6). Kant maintained that this was not a genuine legal order but a Hobbesian state of nature torn apart by perpetual wars.

In order to confront the violence and lawlessness that characterised existing relations between states, Kant reconstructed the cosmopolitan ideal already established as a *moral* norm within the frame of Enlightenment thought (Schlereth 1997). He turned it into a new form of social contract at the inter-state level that placed a political demand on sovereigns to renounce their 'savage and lawless freedom' and submit themselves to public coercive laws. He construed cosmopolitanism as an international political order designed to establish 'lawful external relations among states' and a 'universal civic society'. These terms referred to the establishment or consolidation of international laws to guarantee the sovereignty of nation-states, prohibit interference in the internal affairs of other states and create peaceful relations among states. It also referred to what Kant called cosmopolitan right in the proper sense of the term, which he identified with the 'right of hospitality' belonging to strangers in a foreign land (Kant 1991: 47, 172).[2] He called for the establishment of an 'external legal authority' capable of forcing states to abide by the law and respect the rights of other states, since without this authority every state could simply interpret and enforce international laws according to their own moral or political judgement.

For Kant the three legs of the cosmopolitan condition were international law, cosmopolitan rights and an authoritative international authority. Kant was opposed to the formation of a 'world state', akin to the Leviathan at the intra-societal level, which in his view would either be a 'counterfeit' concealing the rule of a single great power or turn into a 'universal despotism' and 'graveyard of freedom'. The institutional vision he embraced was that of a Federation of Nations, based on mutual co-operation and voluntary consent among a plurality of independent states (Kant 1991: 105, 114). It was a vision far closer to that of our United Nations.

The primary aim of the cosmopolitan condition, as Kant saw it, is to put an end to war between states and establish perpetual peace.

Seeing war as the most serious threat to republican liberty, he envisaged a pacific future in which standing armies would be abolished,
no national debt would be incurred in connection with military
costs and no state would forcibly interfere in the internal affairs
of another. Prior to the attainment of perpetual peace, the cosmopolitan order would establish provisional laws of war. They would
abolish the traditional right of sovereigns to declare war without
consulting their subjects, since citizens who are 'co-legislative members of the state' must give their consent to any declaration of war,
and they would stipulate that wars must be conducted in accordance
with principles which leave states with the possibility of still entering a 'state of right' after the war. They would criminalise acts of war
which 'make mutual confidence impossible during a future time of
peace' and they would preclude wars of extermination and enslave-
ment, the ransom of prisoners, and any use of violence that renders
the perpetrators of violence unfit to be citizens (Kant 1991: 166).

If colonisation was justified by its beneficiaries in terms of 'bringing culture to uncivilised peoples' and purging the home country of
'depraved characters', an improbable combination, Kant argued this
could provide no justification for the plunder, slavery and extermination that typically accompany the acquisition of colonies (Kant
1991: 173). Instead of treating the 'condition of universal hospitality' as a justification for the subjugation of indigenous peoples
by their European conquerors, as Francisco de Vitoria had done in
the sixteenth century on the grounds that Indians had mistreated
European 'travellers', Kant turned the right of hospitality into an
indictment of 'the inhospitable conduct of the civilised states of our
continent ... in visiting foreign countries and peoples (which in
their case is the same as conquering them)'.

Looking back over 200 years later at Kant's cosmopolitanism, it
is difficult not to be impressed by the prescience of his normative
vision. In his pre-revolutionary essay *Idea for a Universal History
from a Cosmopolitan Point of View* (1785), he acknowledged that
cosmopolitanism was a 'fantastical idea' without precedent in world
history. In his post-revolutionary essay *Perpetual Peace* (1795) he
acknowledged that European states were relating to one another
more like atomised individuals in a Hobbesian state of nature than
in accordance with the cosmopolitan ideas which had momentarily lit up the dawn of the French Revolution.[3] In the aftermath of

the Revolution it seemed that nationalism and xenophobia were the rising stars of the new order but Kant's obstinacy lay in trying to harmonise the principle on which the world revolution was turning, the sovereignty of the nation-state, with that of an enlightened rights-based universalism.

Kant maintained that the duty to act in accordance with the idea of perpetual peace was incumbent upon rulers however great the sacrifice they had to make, and upon the people whether or not public opinion recognised it. All politics, Kant declared, must 'bend the knee before right' even if there were not the slightest possibility of its realisation (Kant 1991: 125). Reason, he declared, 'absolutely condemns war' and makes the achievement of peace an 'immediate duty'. That there should be no war is the 'irresistible veto' of the reason within us (Kant 1991: 164, 174). Such moral certainty was, for Kant, unshakeable by experience. Experience could not be a guide to action since it would mean only that those states which most prospered under current arrangements would elevate existing norms as the general standard.

Whilst Kant acknowledged that immediate circumstances were hostile to cosmopolitan ideas, he looked to long-term historical tendencies to defend the *realism* of his vision. He advanced three main lines of argument. They pertained first to the *economic rationality* of cosmopolitanism in a commercial age in which peaceful exchange is more profitable than plunder; second to the *political utility* of cosmopolitanism for states forced to arm themselves against other states and confronted by escalating risks and costs of modern warfare; and third to the *affinity of cosmopolitanism* to *republicanism* given that republican rulers could no longer declare war without consulting their citizens and that republican citizens could be expected to have a higher level of political education and maturity than the subjects of old monarchical states. Kant discerned an affinity between modernity itself and cosmopolitanism, since the modern world is one in which 'the peoples of the earth have entered in varying degrees into a universal community' and 'a violation of rights in one part of the world is felt everywhere' (Kant 1991: 107–8). In this sense it seemed that cosmopolitanism had history on its side.

Kant recognised that there were countervailing tendencies. He acknowledged, for instance, that republican citizens are often civilised 'only in respect of outward courtesies and proprieties' and that militarism can quickly corrupt the mind. Yet the regulative idea that informed his cosmopolitan point of view was that the 'germ of enlightenment' works towards a universal end, 'the perfect civil union of humankind', and that 'genuine principles of right' point towards a 'universal law of humanity' (Kant 1991: 114). Behind the backs of warring humanity he perceived Providence and the Laws of Nature accomplishing their universal purpose. 'Perpetual peace', as Kant put it, 'is *guaranteed* by no less an authority than the great artist *Nature* herself' (Kant 1991: 108).

The cosmopolitan point of view Kant reconstructed was not so much a blueprint for a future interstate order as an elaboration of what human freedom makes possible even at the level of interstate relations. Humanity, he wrote, is 'by its very nature capable of constant progress and improvement without forfeiting its strength . . . no one can or ought to decide what the highest degree may be at which mankind may have to stop progressing, and hence how wide a gap may still of necessity remain between the idea and its execution. For this will depend on freedom, which can transcend any limit we care to impose' (Kant 1991: 189–91). The boldness of Kant's vision was matched by his recognition that the way things are is not the way they have to be and the way things appear is not what they essentially are. However, Kant addressed the limits of natural law from within the frame of natural law and on the margins of his own texts we can detect his apprehension that the cosmopolitan point of view might not provide the necessary solution. Nowhere is this more evident than in his analysis of the rights of man.

The idea of 'the rights of man' was the distinctive accomplishment of eighteenth-century republicanism. It signified that every man should be conceived as a bearer of rights simply by virtue of the fact that he is a man. It contrasted with traditional societies in which the idea of personality, that is, the ability to possess rights, was a privileged status distinct from that of the majority of the population. Roman law distinguished between the status of persons, those who had the right to have rights, and that of slaves and other dependants. The 'rights of man' universalised the status of the person, so that every man was deemed a bearer of rights by virtue of their manhood. Eighteenth-century republicanism then provided the framework in which struggles for the rights of slaves, women, workers and colonial subjects (as well as children, the mad and the bad) could be attached to the original republican conception of 'man'.

No sooner was the idea of the rights of man articulated than it came into conflict with the national organisation of modern political community. While the republican constitution posited the rights of man, it also designated that the nation grants these rights and in its more radical form it declared that no rights are valid which the nation has not granted. The mediation of the nation between 'man' and his rights generated a tension between the universality of the concept and its particular national existence.[4] The slippage from a republican to national conception of popular sovereignty may be illustrated through the experience of the French Revolution. In the early stages of the Revolution the 'sovereignty of the nation' was an index of the struggle for popular sovereignty and there was a notable lack of nationalist sentiment. Decrees were passed offering French citizenship to all foreigners who had resided in France for five years as long as they had means of subsistence; foreign societies and newspapers were encouraged; the use of force against other nations was disavowed; support was given to revolutionaries in other countries to rid themselves of their own rulers; and certain 'benefactors of mankind' (Tom Paine, Mary Wollstonecraft, William Wilberforce, Jeremy Bentham) were awarded honorary French citizenship. This cosmopolitan moment soon evaporated as revolutionary wars were launched, foreigners were held responsible for military defeats, economic problems and political crises, and terror was directed against foreigners. Foreign clubs and newspapers were disbanded and even Tom Paine, 'citizen of the world', was imprisoned and then expelled (Kristeva 1991).

Kantian cosmopolitanism was a profound attempt to address the contradiction between the universalism of the 'rights of man' and the national basis on which rights were accorded. It looked to the generalisation of republican forms of government across all political communities, so that the universality of the rights of man could become a reality; to the development of international law and establishment of a Federation of Nations to ensure that wars between states, perceived as the major threat to the rights of man, could be regulated and eventually overcome; and to cosmopolitan rights in the strict sense of the term to provide a universalistic minimum for 'strangers' and fill the gap in the system of rights left open by international law. However, none of these moves is unproblematic. First, republicanism itself can be an unreliable ally. The inversion of the rights of man into a duty of unconditional obedience to the state which grants these rights creates an internal dynamic towards legal authoritarianism on the part of the state and unthinking patriotism on the part of the citizenry. Second, the generalisation of republicanism across all nations can take the form of war – and war, as Goya's images of 'the disasters of war' illustrate, runs roughshod over the rights of man. Third, the establishment of a Federation of Nations may not provide the alchemy Kant hoped for – that of transforming perpetual war into perpetual peace and lawlessness into the rule of international law – for an alliance of states can construct its own enemies, as can an individual state. Finally, while the idea of cosmopolitan right upholds the right of strangers to 'hospitality', either there is merely a moral injunction on states to respect this right or an international authority would have to possess the means of coercing states to respect them. History can play tricks on all conceptions of human progress and Kant's cosmopolitanism was no exception.

HEGEL'S CRITIQUE OF KANT'S COSMOPOLITANISM

Theodor Adorno's remark that Hegel's 'doctrine of the popular spirit' was nationalistic and reactionary in relation to Kant's cosmopolitanism expresses a very widely held view (Adorno 1990: 309). Following Adorno, Jürgen Habermas identifies the name of Hegel with the prevailing belief in the nineteenth century that 'the political substance and world historical vocation of sovereign nation-states could not be tamed by law' and he quotes Hegel's *Philosophy of Right* to this effect: 'The nation-state is the spirit in its substantial rationality and immediate actuality, and is therefore the absolute power on earth' (Habermas 2006: 151). Habermas argues that Hegel takes aim at the idea of perpetual peace through a confederation of states on the grounds that conflicts between sovereign states can be settled only by war and that the state is not to be understood as existing for the sake of its citizens but as an organic entity and end in itself. There is no shortage of attempts to paint Hegel's philosophy of right in these étatist colours – whether from the point of view of liberal rights theory or critical theory. This conventional reading is, however, misplaced and loses sight, in particular, of the centrality of Hegel's critique of natural law (Rose 1981; Fine 2001a).

Hegel recognised the strength of Kant's cosmopolitan vision. It indicated in his view that Kant had 'some inkling of the nature of spirit . . . to assume a higher shape than that in which its being originally consisted' and he dismissed those critics of cosmopolitanism for whom spirit remained an 'empty word' (Hegel 1991: §343R). Hegel echoed Kant in declaring it a matter of 'infinite importance' that 'a human being counts as such because he is a human being, not because he is a Jew, Catholic, Protestant, German, Italian, etc.' He deemed this idea inadequate '*only* if it adopts a fixed position – for example, as *cosmopolitanism* – in opposition to the concrete life of the state' (Hegel 1991: §209R). It is this inadequacy we need to unpack.

Hegel rejected the dualism Kant sets up between the perpetual violence of the 'Westphalian' past and the perpetual peace of the cosmopolitan future. Looking back he observed that those same natural law jurists whom Kant lumped together as apologists for military aggression (Grotius, Pufendorf and the rest) were the first to give the world anything like a regular system of natural jurisprudence, the first to conceive of the unity of the human race in spite of its division into nations, the first to argue that human unity was a natural law even if it went unacknowledged by those who held that the duties of humanity ought to be conferred on compatriots alone. They did not simply abandon traditional ideas of 'just war' but recast them in terms of the idea of 'right': war could be waged only by a legitimate sovereign state, it had to have good cause, it had to set peace as its end; every state had the right of self-defence, third parties were entitled to help abused states, and barbarous methods of fighting were unlawful.[5] *Ius gentium* stood for a law of nations that was binding despite the absence of higher external authority. As Hegel commented, the principle of international law was that contracts and treaties had to be respected, states had to recognise one another reciprocally as sovereign states, and the conduct of war had to be such as to preserve the possibility of a future peace between sovereign states (Hegel 1991: §333). For Hegel, the crucial point was this: states are no more private persons outside of the society of states than are individuals private persons outside of society:

> Each state is . . . a sovereign and independent entity in relation
> to others . . . and [has] absolute entitlement to be a sovereign
> and independent power *in the eyes of others, i.e. to be recognised*
> by them . . . Without relations with other states, the state can no
> more be an actual individual than an individual can be an actual
> person without a relationship with other persons.
>
> (Hegel 1991: §331)

When Napoleon declared that 'the French Republic is no more in need of recognition than the sun is', this illusion of self-sufficiency proved to be his undoing.[6] *Ius gentium* looked to the construction of a universal concept of humanity as the regulative idea guiding relations between states. Pufendorf treated every society as a 'single person with intelligence and will' but also as moral personalities with civil obligations to one another. Christian Wolff declared the absurdity of seeing the establishment of particular societies as eradicating the universality of human society:

> Just as in the human body individual organs do not cease to
> be organs of the whole human body . . . so likewise individual
> men do not cease to be members of that great society which is
> made up of the whole human race, because several have formed
> together a certain particular society.
>
> (cited in Pagden 2000: 14)

Wolff looked to Europe as 'a kind of republic whose independent members are all linked by common interests' and as the forerunner of a time when 'the voice of nature will reach the civilised peoples of the world and they will realise that all men are brothers'. Emeric de Vattel subordinated any particular society to 'the ties of the universal society which nature has established among men' and looked to commerce and communication as the media through which *civitas maxima* could be established: 'The nations of the world would communicate their goods and their understanding. A profound peace would reign over the earth . . . There would be no more violent means for resolving such differences which might arise. They would all be solved by moderation, justice and equity. The world would seem like one great republic' (cited in Pagden 2000: 11–16).[7]

Perhaps Kant shared the dream of many modern intellectuals, a dream transformed into a political method by the French Revolution, that the rational way of dealing with problems is to 'sweep away the inherited clutter from traditions, clean the slate and start again from scratch' (Toulmin 1992: 175). In the Preface to his *Philosophy of Right* Hegel wrote of those philosophers who imagined that:

> no state or constitution had ever existed or were in existence today, but that we had now (and this 'now' is of indefinite duration) to start right from the beginning, and that the ethical world had been waiting only for such intellectual constructions.
>
> (Hegel 1991: 12)

Whether or not Hegel had Kant in mind, his own account of natural law introduces a historical consciousness of reason that is missing in Kant's moral conception of the past.

Hegel located 'Westphalia' within the wider process of Reformation and the liberation of political life from the control of the Catholic Church. The Reformation introduced the principle that law and government must accord with the idea of free will and that humanity is in its nature destined to be free. Blind obedience to divine law was replaced by the principle of obedience to the laws of the state as the rational element in human will. In practice this meant that the executive powers that were previously the property of dynastic families were gradually transferred into state property. The privileges of the feudal nobility were curtailed and their authority transformed into official positions connected with the state. The dependence of the people on their noble masters was broken and replaced by dependence on the state. Feudal retinues were replaced by standing armies established to supply monarchs with the forces needed for the defence of their states against attacks by foreign enemies and rebellions by their subjects. From wars between states there arose a common interest among all states to preserve their independence but the balance of power between them was continually threatened and the resulting imbalances led to a condition of absolute mistrust. This culminated in the Thirty Years War and scenes of utter desolation in which all the contending forces were wrecked. The Peace of Westphalia brought to a close this condition of perpetual war by establishing a legal framework which recognised the independence of the Protestant Church, ratified the coexistence of religious parties and established a system of rights between states based on human will and empirical observation rather than divine command or revelation. It put an end to religious wars by excluding the religious point of view from international politics and recognising the principle of pluralism among states – or at least among European states (Hegel 1956: 412–57).

Looking forward Hegel questioned the affinity Kant saw between republicanism and perpetual peace – an affinity which led him to understand war as the result of either the backwardness of non-republican states or the lack of a legal framework in interstate relations or both. Hegel was less confident about the pacific quality of republicanism and had some hard-nosed observations to make. First, in republican states responsibility for making war and peace and for the command of armed forces generally lies not with the people but with a 'supreme commander'. The consent of representative institutions may be required for the state to go to war or to secure financing for war, but in any event the people may be more prone to martial enthusiasm than their rulers.[8] Second, there is an affinity between republicanism and patriotic fervour based on the rationality of republican institutions and popular identification with them:

> Patriotism . . . is merely a consequence of the institutions within the state, a consequence in which rationality is *actually* present, just as rationality receives its practical application through action in conformity with the state's institutions . . . This disposition is in general one of trust . . . or the consciousness that my substantial and particular interest is preserved and contained in the interest and end of another (in this case, the state) and in the latter's relation to me as an individual. As a result, this other (the state) immediately ceases to be an other for me, and in my consciousness of this I am free.
>
> (Hegel 1991: §268)

People may convince themselves that their patriotism means 'a willingness to perform *extraordinary* sacrifices and actions' but patriotism is essentially a disposition to trust the state and identify with it (Hegel 1991: §268R). Third, in times of war, when 'the state as such and its independence are at risk', popular identification with the state is intensified and citizens are readier to sacrifice their own individuality to the individuality of the state. Self-sacrifice may appear as an act of individual courage but it remains 'sacrifice in the service of the state' (Hegel 1991: §327A). In war the individual counts merely as 'one among many' and he must bow before the demands of military discipline.[9] He experiences 'the harshness of extreme opposites':

> supreme self-sufficiency ... and total obedience and renuncia-
> tion of personal opinion and reasoning ... personal absence of
> mind, alongside the most intense and comprehensive presence
> of mind ... the most hostile and hence most personal action
> against individuals along with a completely indifferent or even
> benevolent attitude towards them as individuals.
>
> (Hegel 1991: §328)

'Alienation as the existence of freedom': this is how Hegel charac-terises the condition of modern warfare. The valour one is required to show is more 'mechanical' than any other way of risking one's life: it is 'not so much the deed of a particular person as that of a member of a whole' and even the hostility the fighter feels is directed 'not against individual persons but against a hostile whole in gen-eral' (Hegel 1991: §328R). Fourth, war can be useful for republican rulers as a means of averting internal unrest and consolidating the internal power of the state: 'Not only do peoples emerge from wars with added strength, but nations troubled by civil dissension gain internal peace as a result of wars with their external enemies' (Hegel 1991: §324 R and A). War can inject vitality into the body politic and elevate the interest of the community as a whole over the private interest of the individual. Unrelieved peace can foster social stagna-tion: people become 'stuck in their ways' and devoted exclusively to private enrichment. And in international relations there is plenty of scope for a state to feel that it has suffered an injury, that this injury comes from another state and that its own welfare and security are at stake. Finally, a voluntary federation of republican states designed to put an end to wars between them cannot provide the alchemy required of it in Kant's cosmopolitan theory. It remains depend-ent on the particular wills of the member states and it would be

capable of constructing its own enemies: 'even if a number of states join together as a family, this league in its individuality must generate opposition and create an enemy'. If agreement is not reached among its member states conflict can again arise and be settled by war (Hegel 1991: §324A).

While Kant turned republicanism and perpetual peace into the pillars of an ideal political order, Hegel maintained that this congruence depended on an idealised view of the modern state. He sought to capture the fetishism this idealised view of the modern state in a severe style. He wrote of the modern state that it is 'the actuality of the ethical idea . . . an absolute and unmoved end in itself . . . the power of reason actualising itself' (Hegel 1991: §257–8); he added that one should 'expect nothing from the state except what is an expression of rationality . . . [and] venerate the state as an earthly divinity' (§272A); he concluded that as individuals we are mere 'moments' in relation to the self-sufficient power of the state and our existence is a matter of 'indifference' compared with that of the state (§145A). As Hegel clearly and explicitly indicated in the Preface to his *Philosophy of Right*, these words (which have shocked generations of scholars) were intended not as statements of his own opinion but to capture the concept of the modern state itself: its megalomania, its pathological belief in itself as an earthly divinity (Fine 2001a: 22–8).

Modern natural law theory was the framework within which the rationalisation of state power was expressed. The formation of the republican state, Kant writes, is a rational necessity everyone must recognise. The unilateral will of the property owners must give way to a 'collective, universal and powerful Will that can provide the guarantees required' (Kant 1965: §8). People must be *forced* into the state if they fail to do so of their own accord. Once they have entered into this 'civil condition' their absolute obligation is to obey the law of the state. The duty of the citizen is to 'endure even the most intolerable abuse of supreme authority' since the 'well-being of the state' refers only to that condition in which 'the constitution conforms most closely to the principles of justice' and must not be confused with 'the welfare or happiness of the citizens of the state' (Kant 1965: 86). The state legislature can do 'absolutely no injustice to anyone' and while citizens can lodge complaints about unjust laws they must not disobey them. It is 'the people's duty to endure even the most intolerable abuse of supreme authority' (Kant 1965: 86). While citizens have the right and duty to think for themselves, this right and duty is restricted to 'the use which anyone may make of it as a man of learning addressing the entire reading public' (Kant 1991: 55). Otherwise, as in the case of an officer receiving a command from his superiors or a clergyman receiving an order from the church, we must obey. The freedom of citizens does not lie in their capacity to choose for or against the law but only in their 'internal legislation of reason' (Kant 1965: 28).

There was more to Kant's political philosophy than this: he advanced the idea of moral laws as laws of autonomy which individuals impose on themselves; he recognised that 'the good attains the "highest good" only when it is realised in external reality'; he guaranteed to individuals a maximum of rights compatible with the rights of others; he celebrated the courage to think for oneself and called upon citizens to express their reason in public fora. And yet – and this I take to be the nub of Hegel's critique – Kant's critical philosophy turns out not to be critical enough. State-consciousness haunts the antechambers of his discussion of republicanism, since his concern is to rediscover the idea of right in every sphere of private, public and interstate law he depicts. He gives a roughly accurate empirical account of power in modern republican states, only to convert these empirical facts into postulates of practical reason.[10] The suspicion Hegel expresses is that once we explore the substance of the republican state – the power of its executive, its propensities to legal authoritarianism, the patriotism it fosters, the disciplinary powers it wields, the interests of its rulers in war, its view of itself as an Earthly God – the affinity between republicanism and cosmopolitanism becomes more problematic. The lesson we can draw from Hegel's critique of Kant's cosmopolitanism is that war between states is the product not only of the backwardness of non-republican states or the lawlessness of interstate relations but of the form of the modern state itself.

VIOLENCE AND THE MODERN STATE

In his relation to Kant Hegel did not attempt to wipe the slate clean as Kant did vis-à-vis the preceding tradition of natural law. He certainly did not stand for the reinstatement of the rule of power and contingency in our conceptual framework: 'it is not just the power of spirit which passes judgement in world history . . . it is not the abstract and irrational necessity of a blind fate' (Hegel 1991: §342). While he recognised the ethical nature of Kant's project, to harmonise liberal republicanism with the idea of a cosmopolitan order, he sought to draw it out of a natural law framework and into the real world of conflicting social forms.

Freedom, Kant wrote, 'can transcend any limit we care to impose'. He placed cosmopolitanism within a progressive philosophy of history. However, Hegel observed, the freedom to transcend every limit also has a negative, destructive aspect. To paraphrase Marx, it can turn all that is solid into air, profane all that is holy, sweep away ancient and venerable prejudices and newly formed opinions before they can ossify. It can devalue all established values. Freedom beyond all limits, Hegel wrote, is 'the freedom of the void'. Triggered by the conjunction of absolute freedom and terror in the French Revolution, Hegel saw in this event the signs of an organised violence to come, distinct from conventional wars between states. He often tried to formulate what was original about this violence and here is an extract from one well-known example in the *Philosophy of Right*:

> This was a time of trembling and quaking and of intolerance towards everything particular. For fanaticism wills only what is abstract, not what is articulated, so that whenever differences emerge, it finds them incompatible with its own indeterminacy and cancels them. This is why the people, during the French revolution, destroyed once more the institutions they had themselves created, because all institutions are incompatible with the abstract self-consciousness of equality.
>
> (Hegel 1991: §5R and A)

Hegel argued that where the essential element of freedom appears as the possibility of abstracting from every determination in which I find myself, what is left is only the 'freedom of the void'. Raised to the status of an actual shape and passion in the realm of politics and religion, such freedom expresses itself in a fury of destruction, for it is only in destroying something that this negative will has a feeling of its own existence. It may believe it wills some positive condition, such as universal equality or a new world order, but its negative consciousness demands the annihilation of every objective determination. Self-determination becomes 'sheer restless activity which cannot yet arrive at something *that is*' (Hegel 1991: §108A). This violence, with its resonances of a totalitarianism to come, reveals the one-sidedness of linking liberal republicanism too closely to ideas of peace and freedom. The form of the modern state also has an internal relationship to a politics that is at once destructive and nihilistic. Perhaps this is the nub of Hegel's criticism of Kant: we cannot simply ratchet cosmopolitan laws and institutions onto existing forms of the modern state and think we have solved the problem of political violence. Cosmopolitanism has to be more transformative than this.

3

COSMOPOLITANISM AND POLITICAL COMMUNITY[1]
The equivocations of constitutional patriotism

The daunting problem any cosmopolitan faces is how to understand the relation between cosmopolitanism as a transformative project and actually existing forms of political community. The new cosmopolitanism characteristically pursues a middle path between two extremes: one is 'the end of the nation-state' thesis and its displacement by global forms of political community; the other is the reconciliation of cosmopolitanism with the existing nation-state. In place of both extremes the new cosmopolitanism usually conceives the 'cosmopolitan condition' as a multilayered global order consisting of a reformed basis of solidarity within the nation-state, the development of transnational forms of political community such as the European Union with new forms of solidarity to match, and the consolidation of international institutions, movements and laws regulating relations between states and guaranteeing the rights and freedoms of global citizens. It treats this multilayered order not only as something to be desired but as a visible development albeit one contested from both ends of the political spectrum and in need of nurturing in its own right. The cosmopolitan condition from this perspective is a differentiated architectonic of legal and political forms and cosmopolitanism is a way of seeing and acting in relation to this complexity. This understanding of the relation between cosmopolitanism as a transformative project and existing forms of political community is the subject matter of this chapter.

I am not going to start from scratch. In contemporary social theory it is in the work of Jürgen Habermas that we find a sustained and intellectually rich attempt to address these issues, and it is through an engagement with Habermas that I propose to proceed. I treat Habermas as a sophisticated and thoughtful exemplar of the new cosmopolitanism who gives to the general approach his own distinctive slant. Habermas is deeply indebted to Kant. He maintains that the challenges posed by the catastrophes of the twentieth century and the forces of globalisation have given new impetus to Kant's idea of a cosmopolitan condition. He recognises that today we cannot simply echo Kant's eighteenth-century vision. We have to 'iron out its inconsistencies', radicalise its break from the old order of nation-states, draw out the connections between peace and social justice, overcome its metaphysical assumptions and generally take account of the differences in both global situation and conceptual framework that now separate us from him (Habermas 1997). Habermas's intuition, however, is that Kant's conception of the 'cosmopolitan condition' remains a vital resource for our own times, and in this spirit he offers a prime example of what Karl-Otto Apel has called 'thinking with Kant against Kant' (Apel 1997: 87).

Whilst I have much sympathy with Habermas's proposals, they also give expression to the difficulties cosmopolitan authors face in trying to break free of the natural law framework and the temptations which lead them to import a series of questionable idealisations into their theories. Challenging the 'idealisations' attendant in cosmopolitan conceptions of political community, I would wish to re-emphasise the role of political judgement on the part of ordinary citizens.

CONSTITUTIONAL PATRIOTISM AND COSMOPOLITANISM

The solution Habermas offers to the problem of reconciling cosmopolitanism as a transformative project with existing forms of political community is more ambiguous than it might at first appear. A distinctively cosmopolitan accent is to be found in his appeal to the historical contingency of the nation-state as the exclusive organising basis for political communities, the death of nationalism as a normative basis for social integration, and the necessity of cosmopolitan justice occasioned by new global risks and pressures. However, Habermas maintains that the tension between the nation-state and cosmopolitanism can be overstated and that respect for constitutionally regulated processes of national politics can be reconciled with the authority of cosmopolitan institutions. This outcome is possible if cosmopolitan institutions enforce the same principles of justice as those that regulate politics at a national level. Only if politics at a national level express radically different principles of justice from those that regulate cosmopolitan institutions – if, for example, a nation-state is based on ethnic principles and authorises major human rights violations against its own population – only then will the conditions for conflict be acute. Habermas's strategy is to look for reconciliation between national and cosmopolitan institutions, supplemented by the imposition of cosmopolitan law (by force if necessary) where the possibility of reconciliation is absent.

Habermas reserves the word 'nationalism' (as opposed to patriotism) for a regressive credo that unreflectively celebrates the history, destiny, culture or blood of a nation. At the same time he emphatically affirms the legitimacy of 'constitutional patriotism' and its fit with cosmopolitan thinking. Habermas is well aware that the historical strength of nationalist sentiment is due to its capacity to act as a binding power enabling individuals to coalesce around commonly shared symbols and ideologies, and that the formation of the modern nation-state has been dependent on the development of a national consciousness to provide it with 'the cultural substrate for a civil solidarity'. Today he presents constitutional patriotism as the particular type of national consciousness most appropriate to nation-states seeking to inspire rational loyalty on the part of their citizens (Habermas 2001a: 64). If some kind of national consciousness is required from the point of view of inculcating a willingness on the part of citizens to do what is required of them for the common good, such as the maintenance of public services through taxation or the acceptance of democratic decisions as legitimate, it is according to Habermas constitutional patriotism that can perform these integrative functions in ways compatible with cosmopolitan forms of life.

The constitution serves here as a bridge between the universal and the particular. On the one hand, constitutional patriotism refers to a shared attachment towards universalistic principles implicit in the idea of constitutional democracy. On the other hand, popular attachment to the idea of a constitution entails the sense of attachment citizens feel towards the particular ways in which abstract principles are interpreted and applied through national institutions. Frank Michelman places particular stress on this national aspect: constitutional patriotism is 'a disposition of attachment to one's country, specifically in view of a certain spirit sustained by the country's people and their leaders in debating and deciding disagreements of essential constitutional import' (Michelman 2001: 265). Habermas is equally at pains to emphasise the national content of constitutional patriotism:

> The political culture of a country crystallizes around its constitution. Each national culture develops a distinctive interpretation of those constitutional principles that are equally embodied in other republican constitutions – such as popular sovereignty and human rights – in light of its own national history. A 'constitutional patriotism' based on these interpretations can take the place originally occupied by nationalism.
>
> (Habermas 1998: 118)

> The universalism of legal principles manifests itself in a procedural consensus, which must be embedded through a kind of constitutional patriotism in the context of a historically specific political culture.
>
> (Habermas 1998: 226)

Constitutional patriotism refers *both* to a shared attachment towards universalistic principles *and* to the actualisation of these principles in the form of particular national institutions. It is this 'both–and' quality that allows constitutional patriotism to nurture a disposition of attachment to one's country and be compatible with the transformed self-consciousness of world citizens.

Because both constitutional patriotism and cosmopolitanism are based on universal principles of right, the possibility of conflict does not disturb the sleep of their advocates. Georg Cavallar, for instance, champions their unity when he writes: 'Only constitutional patriotism is by definition all-inclusive and comprehensive, because it is based on the universal principle of right ... Only constitutional patriotism does not contradict cosmopolitanism' (Cavallar 1999: 143). Habermas balances the constitutional and national aspects of constitutional patriotism thus:

> The political integration of citizens ensures loyalty to the common political culture. The latter is rooted in an interpretation of constitutional principles from the perspective of the nation's historical experience ... These [constitutional principles] form the fixed point of reference for any constitutional patriotism that situates the system of rights within the historical context of a legal community.
>
> (Habermas 1998: 225)

Precisely what is meant by reconciling constitutional principles with the historical experience of a nation is not yet spelt out and the question remains whether this theoretical reconciliation confronts the real dilemmas citizens may face over whether to support their 'own' national interpretation of constitutional principles or accede to a more distant cosmopolitan view. Such a conflict is not hard to envisage, and Habermas illustrates its potential when he draws a strong contrast between Anglo-American and continental-European interpretations of the principles of international law: 'the former resorting to maxims of traditional power politics, the latter appealing to more principled reasons for transforming classical international law into some sort of cosmopolitan order' (Habermas 2001b). Habermas himself refers to what he sees as the distinct traditions of J. S. Mill-style liberal nationalism and Kantian liberal internationalism. The distinction between these traditions indicates exactly the kinds of intellectual and historical resources that might stimulate potentially disturbing conflicts between constitutional patriotism and cosmopolitanism.

The potential for conflict between constitutional patriotism and cosmopolitanism may be concealed for reasons Habermas would not find attractive, namely that we are dealing here with elastic and unstable concepts which make it difficult to render firm conceptual distinctions. If constitutional patriotism is only a shared commitment to the constitutional regulation of power, then it is little wonder that it extends easily across national boundaries. But if it is meant to locate these principles firmly within the corporate identity of a national community, then its extension across national boundaries becomes more challenging and must overcome the national differences that constitute part of its content. Thomas Mertens, for example, argues that without shared understandings and a particular forum within which constitutional powers can be fashioned, there is, properly speaking, no such thing as a political community or culture at all (Mertens 1996: 340). The thrust of this approach is to shore up constitutional principles through the shared sense of attachment that only national communities provide. The problem is that constitutional patriotism may be either too strong or too weak to serve Habermas's purpose. In its strong form it binds the people of a particular nation around their own distinctive interpretations of constitutional principles at the cost of closing them off from effective identification with cosmopolitan considerations. In its weak form it constitutes a simple adherence to formal procedures for the realisation of constitutional principles and fails to establish the ethic of solidarity necessary to facilitate the formation of political community.

CONSTITUTIONAL PATRIOTISM AND GERMAN NATIONALISM

Habermas developed the theory of constitutional patriotism in the German context as a device to integrate pluralistic and multicultural national communities on a rational and lawful basis and provide an antidote to all forms of (ethnic) nationalism.[2] He acknowledged that nationalism might once have provided valuable moral resources for anti-imperialist struggles or the building of welfare states, but he maintained that nationalism can no longer meet the normative requirements of our age. He depicted constitutional patriotism as a self-reflective form of loyalty to the constitutional principles of the state that relativises our own way of life, grants strangers the same rights as ourselves and enlarges tolerance and respect for others. It recognises the necessity of nation-states but also the heterogeneity of their populations. It is inclusive of all citizens regardless of race, colour, creed, gender, language, religion or ethnicity, and the political community it visualises is one of equal rights-bearing individuals united by a shared attachment to constitutional practices and values.

Habermas emphasises the distinction between *constitutional* patriotism and the more traditional forms of patriotism. While patriotism in general may be read as a disposition to trust in and identify with the state, constitutional patriotism demands loyalty only to the constitutional principles of the state and not the state itself. While patriotism in general requires obedience to the law of the land, constitutional patriotism distinguishes between what is law and what is right and mandates that all positive law be evaluated in the light of universal precepts embodied in the constitution. The principles of the constitution stand in for natural law. The critical content of constitutional patriotism is the principle that the state can expect obedience to its law only if it rests on principles worthy of recognition. Habermas portrays the idea of the constitution as the '*terminus ad quem* of the process of juridification of political power' (Habermas 2006: 131). He presents it as the form of law that 'a community of free and equal citizens gives itself' and distinguishes it sharply from the state: whilst the state is a 'complex of hierarchically organised capacities available for the exercise of political power', the constitution is a 'horizontal association of citizens' constructed by 'laying down the fundamental rights that free and equal founders mutually grant each other'. In short, Habermas presents the constitution as the apex of the 'republican transformation of state power by law': the apex because it finally reverses the initial situation in which 'law serves as an instrument of power' (Habermas 2006: 131–2).

The idealisation of the constitution draws its persuasiveness from the role of the constitution in regulating the power of the state, specifying its division of powers, guaranteeing the rights of individuals and articulating the underlying values the state purports to uphold. However, behind the appearance of a *free* constitution we still encounter a *definite* constitution – one which is not a matter of free choice but, as Hegel once put it, 'accords with the national spirit at a given stage of its development' (Hegel 1975: 123). The constitution is not only the organising principle of the modern state but is also one element in the complex organism of the political state as a whole. As such, it exists alongside the other elements of the state – notably, the sovereign, the representative assembly, the executive and the judiciary. The modern state is a complex and differentiated organism and its various powers acquire their individual significance through the functions they perform in relation to one another. The constitution not only guarantees rights and inhibits power but it also (to paraphrase Hegel and Marx) allows for change only in so far as it is tranquil, prevents people from crystallising into a powerful opposition to the organised state and constitutes the sacred element of the state apparently exalted above the sphere of contingency and human agency (Hegel 1991: §273–302). The question I would address, therefore, is whether constitutional patriotism affords to the constitution an aura of freedom that is difficult to square with the actual constitution imposed on post-1945 Germany by the victorious powers, which contained the right of return for ethnic Germans and provided a focal point around which a broad political coalition afraid of radical change coalesced. To be sure, these attributes are not at all attractive to Habermas, whose decoupling of state and nation explicitly called into question the West German Basic Law and its *volkish* conception of citizenship, but they highlight the difficulty of setting the constitution over and above the formation of the state as a whole.[3]

There is a curiously German inflection to the theory of constitutional patriotism. If it is true, as Habermas was not alone in thinking, that Germany emerged on the basis of a *volkish* conception of the nation and became the standard bearer of romantic nationalism, Habermas reverses all that and in his thought post-war Germany takes over the torch of enlightenment (Meinecke 1977). Germany appears as an exemplary nation in the sense that it has 'learnt' from history of the dangers of a non-rational sense of political belonging and has adopted 'a postnational self-understanding of the political community' (Habermas 1998: 119). In a paradoxical moment Habermas presents Germany as the European nation that, because of its own nationalist excesses and the painful memories that ensued, most fully acknowledges nationalism as the 'terrible, horrific regression' that it is. In Germany national identity can be rebuilt only through a sense of joint responsibility among Germans to keep alive the memory of those murdered by German hands, a responsibility which carries over into next generations. Constitutional patriotism finds a special home in Germany for the German condition highlights the essential lesson of twentieth-century history – that nationalism is no longer defensible as an ethical ideal. From the point of view of one brought up in post-war England, where the British war effort was highly praised in nationalistic terms, it may appear that Habermas had a point.

The paradoxical sense of German pride Habermas gives to the theory of constitutional patriotism, a pride in having learnt from history, carries with it an equivalent sense of guilt for those who still think in nationalist terms. Habermas not only distinguished constitutional patriotism analytically from nationalism, he also treated nationalism as one of the pathologies of modern society. The theory of constitutional patriotism declares that a key political struggle of our age is between those who believe that their nation should be based on universal constitutional principles and those who still base their nation on ethnic or at least culturally specific membership. If all nationalism is Janus-faced, containing within itself both the values and the barbarities of the idea of national self-determination, Habermas puts all that is positive on the side of constitutional patriotism and all that is negative on the side of nationalism. This conceptual dichotomy, however, splits the good from the bad without confronting the equivocations of nationalism as such. The risk of such an approach is that it constructs a moral division of the world between us and them, friend and enemy, constitutional patriot and nationalist, that stigmatises the other as much as it idealises itself.

This dualistic way of thinking has echoes of an old Marxism that made equally categorical distinctions between the 'nationalism of the oppressed' and the 'nationalism of the oppressor'. This opposition was originally rooted in the division of the world between colonising and colonised countries but came to be an organising principle of Marxist political thought that made arbitrary distinctions based on all manner of contingent factors, especially the relation of this or that nationalism to Russian foreign policy imperatives (Rodinson 1972). The dichotomy between nationalism and constitutional patriotism is, of course, conceptually quite different from the dichotomy between the nationalisms of the oppressor and of the oppressed, one based on content and the other on form, but in both cases we find ourselves immersed in a prior settlement that creates its own notions of superiority and inferiority. I do not claim that constitutional patriotism *must be* exclusionary in this way – only that the urge is internal to it (Mehta: 1999). These observations are not intended to support a light-minded relativism, as if there were nothing to choose between nationalism and constitutional patriotism, but to open up a more troubling vista: that constitutional patriotism is closer to nationalism than its advocates would like to think and its compatibility with cosmopolitanism less secure. It is perhaps this sense of unease over the affinity of constitutional patriotism to nationalism that led Habermas to relocate the theory on a transnational stage.

CONSTITUTIONAL PATRIOTISM AND THE TURN TO EUROPE

Faced with the difficulties of reconciling cosmopolitanism with constitutional patriotism at the level of the nation-state, Habermas turns to the idea of the transnational political community and the European Union in particular as a functional equivalent to the nation-state in a postnational age. His remark that 'national politics have dwindled to more or less intelligent management of a process of forced adaptation to the pressure to shore up purely local positional advantages', may be taken as exemplary of the reduction he sees in the nation-state's own functional capacities (Habermas 2001a: 61). Habermas advanced a number of persuasive pragmatic arguments in favour of this transnational turn. He suggests, for example, that transnational mechanisms of governance are more capable than national governments of constructing a life-world response to the systemic forces of globalisation, more capable of integrating 'mixed' populations with a self-awareness of their own cultural diversity, and more capable of overcoming the kind of nationalism that led to two world wars, the mass production of displaced persons and the rise of national socialism.

To be sure, the pragmatic arguments for the transnational turn are all contestable. First, the formation of a transnational body such as the European Union may be a necessary condition for responding politically to globalising systemic pressures but it is not sufficient. Some conservatives who share Habermas's enthusiasm for the political integration of the European Union do so for opposite reasons: they applaud the fact that the EU is functionally driven and erodes inhibitions imposed by nation-states on the movement of capital. Conversely, the normative presupposition of some social democrats opposed to the political integration of the European Union is that social democracy is only realisable through the institutions of the nation-state. Second, the theory of constitutional patriotism itself reveals, the modern idea of the nation is no less artificial than the idea of the transnational political community. Both create political unity among rights-bearing citizens from diverse backgrounds and it is not self-evident that a multicultural nation-state is less capable of providing a political form appropriate to the heterogeneity of populations than a transnational political community. Third, totalitarian movements in the mid-twentieth century were not in any strict sense nationalistic. They represented a reactionary form of revolt against the whole system of nation-states, they organised on a transnational scale, they had global ambitions, they scorned the parochialism of nationalist ways of thinking, they were bent on the destruction of the institutions of the nation-state, and they thought and acted in terms of racial or class principles that shattered any conventional sense of national unity. The reconstruction of the nation-state could provide, as Talcott Parsons appreciated, as plausible a response to the experience of totalitarianism as the construction of new transnational entities (Chernilo 2007a).

Over and above any such pragmatic considerations Habermas views the extension of constitutional patriotism from the national to the European level not only as providing a rational basis for European political integration but also as furthering the process of separating citizenship from *Volk* that began in the post-war German context. However, the equivocations of transnationalism as a political solution to the problems raised both by globalisation and nationalistic responses to globalisation impelled Habermas to place more weight on the specific idea of 'Europe' to justify the transplantation of constitutional patriotism to this level. Although Habermas envisages the EU as a model for other transnational political communities, he also represents it as occupying its own determinate social and cultural space. Europe, he maintains, supports the re-instatement of the re-distributive policies of the welfare state; Europe permits a close mesh of deliberative politics, civic value orientations and shared conceptions of justice; Europe provides a space in which human rights culture and politics can flourish and in which citizens can see themselves at once as nationals, Europeans and world citizens. The terms that run through his analysis of Europe are those of 'shared values', a 'form of life', a 'model of society', a 'civic tradition', a 'particular ethos', etc. In his essay on 'Why Europe needs a constitution' Habermas argues that the project of European political union requires 'the legitimation of shared values . . . an interest in and affective attachment to a particular ethos . . . the attraction of a particular way of life'. During the third quarter of the past century, he writes, 'the citizens of Western Europe were fortunate enough to develop a distinctive form of life' and today this persists. His sociological faith is that 'against perceived threats from globalisation' the citizens of the EU 'are prepared to defend the core of a welfare state that is the backbone of a society still oriented towards social, political and cultural inclusion'. Europe, in his view, is 'more than a market . . . it stands for a model of society that has grown historically' (Habermas 2001b: 8–10). The 'post-traditional' model of society Habermas sees in Europe has nothing to do with the Carolingian heritage of the founding fathers of Europe with its explicit appeal to a Christian West, nor indeed with any concept of a European nation existing independently of, or prior to, the political process from which it springs. Yet it is precisely this post-traditional quality that distinguishes the European political community from others and makes it special.

The form of life Habermas sees in Europe is one that acknowledges its own deeply equivocal history but stands for normative principles that learn from and confront the dark side of this historical experience. In his earlier writings on Germany, Habermas spoke of the need for a 'critical appropriation of ambiguous traditions' to understand how a civilised nation could be capable of the crimes committed under Nazism and yet recover the tradition of constitutional patriotism inaugurated by Kant. Now he brings the idea of 'critical appropriation' to a larger European canvas. This reconstructive approach is important if we are not simply to impose an abstract 'ought' on Europe but build on what already exists. Yet there is something ambiguous in this 'critical appropriation of ambiguous traditions'. In earlier writings Habermas cited Thomas Mann: 'There are not two Germanys, an evil and a good, but only one which, through devil's cunning, transformed its best into evil'. He also cites Walter Benjamin: 'There has never been an artefact of culture that is not at the same time an artefact of barbarism'. We might add the warning bell rung by Hannah Arendt at the start of her book, *The Origins of Totalitarianism*:

> We can no longer afford to take that which was good in the past and simply call it our heritage, to discard the bad and simply think of it as a dead load which by itself time will bury in oblivion. The subterranean stream of Western history has finally come to the surface and has usurped the dignity of our tradition. This is the reality in which we live.
>
> (Arendt 1979: ix)

To my mind, these quotations go against the grain of simply treating the tradition of 'constitutional patriotism' as the good and calling it our heritage and discarding 'nationalism' as the bad and thinking of it as a dead load. Charles Turner points out that the theory of constitutional patriotism does not easily cohere with 'the view from Eastern Europe' where:

> the source of pain was not 'nationalist excess' alone, but rather six years of Nazi occupation followed by forty years of Soviet domination . . . The lesson of history here is not one in which the mistakes of the past are corrected, but one in which the past continues to haunt the present.
>
> (Turner 2004: 303)

From this perspective Habermas's critical appropriation of ambiguous traditions may appear too quick to 'resolve' the equivocations of the past. He not only faces the sociological question of how far his enlightened vision for Europe is in fact rooted in the social and political consciousness of Europeans, especially given the regression of public opinion into defensive manoeuvres of a nationalistic kind, but also the conceptually more demanding question of whether the postnational vision of Europe represents a kind of nationalism writ large that may not be appealing to all its constituent parts, let alone to those outside its borders. His anti-*Gemeinschaftlich* version of Europe avoids any formulation of European identity along culturally homogeneous lines, but the appeal to a European 'way of life', grounded neither in state power (the medium of the east) nor in money (the medium of the west) but in communicative rationality (the medium of civil society), has an affinity to nationalism – enough at least to question the premature identification of constitutional patriotism with the name of cosmopolitanism.

CONSTITUTIONAL PATRIOTISM AND DEMOCRACY

There is a further issue raised by the turn to Europe that one might expect would make Habermas wary of the transnational turn: it has to do with the question of democracy. For Habermas, constitutional patriotism has a rational content in part because it rests on the twin pillars of human rights and democratic participation. It represents a shared attachment to political procedures that offer citizens the chance to be at the same time recipients and authors of the laws that govern them: bearers of rights and participants in the processes that determine the distribution of rights. In this conception of political community any democratic praxis presupposes participants as bearers of legal rights and any system of rights presupposes that they are legitimated and substantiated through democratic deliberation. Habermas writes:

> The internal relation between democracy and the rule of law consists of this: on the one hand, citizens can make appropriate use of their public autonomy only if, on the basis of their equally protected private autonomy, they are sufficiently independent; on the other hand, they can realise equality in the enjoyment of their private autonomy only if they make appropriate use of their political autonomy as citizens.
>
> (Habermas 2001a: 118)

Within the framework of the nation-state this normative perspective is actualised by the constitutional regulation of power and guarantee of basic rights, the creation of positive laws in the representative assembly, a professional civil service, an impartial judiciary and a healthy civil society and public sphere. The question is whether the co-originality of rights and democracy can hold when we move from a national to transnational frame of reference.

While Habermas is quick to deride the idea that solidarity ties are conceptually linked to a nation-state, he is cautious about breaking the connection between democracy and the nation-state. At times he offers a depiction of democracy that stresses the boundaries of political community within the nation-state: 'democratic self-determination can only come about if the population of a state is transformed into a nation of citizens who take their political destiny into their own hands' (Habermas 2001a: 64). At other times he seems to hold that the attainment of democracy beyond the limits of the nation-state is both a desideratum and real possibility: 'precisely the artificial conditions in which national consciousness arose argue against the defeatist assumption that a form of civic solidarity amongst strangers can only be generated within the confines of the nation' (Habermas 2001a: 102). His understanding of constitutional order, that it is 'a political order created by the people themselves and legitimated by their opinion and will formation', does not presuppose the existence of a nation and leaves the scope of democratic political community undefined providing only that democratic procedures exist to facilitate the legitimate generation of positive law (Habermas 2001a: 65).

One of the problems Habermas has to face in transplanting constitutional patriotism to Europe is the well-worked charge that transnational institutions cannot replicate the democratic legitimacy possible at the national level. Will Kymlicka puts the matter thus: 'transnational organisations exhibit a major "democratic deficit" and have little public legitimacy in the eyes of citizens' (Kymlicka 2001: 312). Habermas acknowledges that in transnational political communities it is harder for individual citizens to relate to authoritative decisions: 'As new organisations emerge even further removed from the political base, such as the Brussels bureaucracy, the gap between self-programming administrations and systemic networks, on the one hand, and democratic processes, on the other, grows constantly' (Habermas 1998: 151). He acknowledges that a democratic deficit emerges because no effective way has yet been discovered to replicate the forms of national democratic deliberation and decision-making at the transnational level. The dilemma it creates for Habermas is that on the one hand he holds that transnational political community is *required* for all the conceptual and practical reasons elaborated above, and on the other that transnational institutions do not easily compete with the democratic legitimacy of national decision-making.

In the face of this dilemma a device Habermas employs is to draw on the two track theory of deliberative democracy he originally devised for national communities. There must be some organic connection between formal processes of democratic will-formation in representative bodies and informal processes of opinion formation within the public sphere – some scope for creative interaction between the two spheres. Civil society must be able to influence, though not coerce, processes of will formation and this influence must go beyond conventional means of participating in elections. One reason why Habermas accords such a significant role to civil society is its *epistemic* function for democracy: 'democratic procedure no longer draws its legitimising force only, indeed not even predominantly, from political participation and the expression of political will, but rather from the general accessibility of a deliberative process whose structure grounds an expectation of rationally acceptable results' (Habermas 2001a: 110). The *rational* quality of outcomes is dependent on a deliberative process sensitive to the communicative power generated at the level of civil society, a power difficult to achieve in the sphere of will formation. This intimate relationship between democratic procedures whose legitimacy rests on the grounds that they are open to all and democratic procedures whose legitimacy rests on the grounds that deliberation and decision-making have a rational quality, helps us understand how Habermas expects transnational bodies to achieve acceptable standards of democratic legitimacy. Even if the deliberative processes of civil society are unable to replicate the legitimacy conferred on nation-states through representative bodies, they may at least be able to mimic the *informal* moment of democratic legitimacy:

> The institutionalised participation of non-governmental organisations in the deliberations of international negotiating systems would strengthen the legitimacy of the procedure insofar as mid-level transnational decision-processes could then be rendered transparent for national public spheres, and thus be reconnected with decision-making procedures at the grassroots level.
>
> (Habermas 2001a: 111)

The strength of this argument lies in the complex view of democratic legitimacy it invokes. However, it downplays the role of representative bodies at the transnational level and suggests that democratic legitimacy at this level can be more of a one track rather than two track process. It may be true, as Habermas claims, that emphasising the rationality of deliberative processes 'loosens the conceptual ties between democratic legitimacy and the familiar forms of state organisation', but loosening the ties is a different matter from breaking them altogether.

The difficulty is this: the larger units of political decision-making required to control global economic forces are those that are likely to have less democratic legitimacy by the standards of democracy Habermas has elaborated in the context of the nation-state. He fore-stalls pessimism by encouraging us to re-conceptualise the European Union through the lens of a *new* kind of democratic political body. Nonetheless, he risks undermining values he wishes to promote, namely those that support a democratic form of political life, by advocating a transnational solution which cannot secure the same degree of democratic legitimacy as the nation-state. Increasingly Habermas seems to handle this problem by emphasising that 'democratic procedures of legitimation ... demand a form of civic solidarity that *cannot* be extended at will beyond the borders of the nation-state' and arguing that, since the EU is not a 'state' in the proper sense of the term and lacks the core element of sovereignty, namely monopoly on the legitimate use of force, it is not subject to the same demanding requirements of democratic legitimacy as the nation-state (Habermas 2006: 139). He seems to reconcile himself to the prospect that, at the transnational level, 'constitutions of the liberal type recommend themselves', that is, a constitutional order only indirectly tied to processes of democratic legitimation.

COSMOPOLITANISM AND NATURAL LAW THEORY

This reconstruction of Habermas's political writings illustrates some of the complexities of adopting a cosmopolitan perspective. It involves three stages of analysis: (a) it traces the shifting basis of solidarity at the national level and extracts from this analysis normative conclusions regarding the decline of nationalism and rise of constitutional patriotism as a form of reflective and critical solidarity justifiable in their own right and compatible with a cosmopolitan political imagination; (b) it traces the conflicts involved in seeking to develop constitutional patriotism at the national level, including the emergence of surrogate forms of nationalism, and the kinds of resolution offered by the development of transnational forms of political community; and (c) it traces the conflicts involved in the development of transnational resolutions in relation to the danger both of constructing a new nationalism writ-large and of not being able to reproduce the degree of democratic legitimacy possible at the national level. In the next chapter I shall pursue this story at the level of international institutions and laws. At this stage, however, we can draw certain conclusions concerning the differentiated character of the 'cosmopolitan condition' and some of the misunderstandings which surround it.

The new cosmopolitanism is not so much about the displacement of the national by the transnational and thence the international but rather about the 'fit' between these levels of political community. It is about the necessity of enlarging our political imagination so as to be able to break from the fetters of nationalism politically and methodologically. The great strength of Habermas is that he locates cosmopolitanism in the world of actually existing political forms and he looks for the real-life bearers of the cosmopolitan project on this terrain. This said, I have tried to show that the fit between constitutional patriotism and cosmopolitanism is more problematic than Habermas allows. There is something about the way Habermas imagines reconciliation that is indicative of the difficulties the new cosmopolitanism has more generally in extracting itself from a natural law framework. Whilst he is not to be faulted for seeing the cosmopolitan condition as a complex and differentiated whole, the reconciliation he offers between cosmopolitanism as a transformative political project and existing political communities hangs on idealisations of the constitution, patriotism and the idea of Europe that rationalise rather than confront the exclusions on which they are based. One of the challenges facing cosmopolitan social theory is how to foster the development of particular forms of political community whilst at the same time resisting the temptation to identify them with the name of cosmopolitanism.

I shall end this chapter with the observation that Habermas self-consciously analyses cosmopolitanism within the framework of natural law theory. This claim may appear surprising given his explicit commitment to overcoming Kantian metaphysics but for Habermas this means modernising natural law theory, not supplanting it. For Kant, as we have seen, the necessity of embracing a cosmopolitan perspective was not accounted for primarily as a political response to social circumstances but as a demand of reason. He deduced cosmopolitanism from the postulates of Practical Reason. Habermas rejects the suggestion that cosmopolitanism can be justified in this way. One of the key problems he sees in Kant's theory of cosmopolitanism is precisely the metaphysical baggage it still carries. Rather than derive the idea of the 'cosmopolitan condition' from a priori principles of right, he introduces the 'postmetaphysical' proposition that if individuals are to be the authors of the laws to which they are subject, then the form and content of these laws have to be determined through intersubjective processes of deliberation. The issue here is one of admitting democratic procedures and non-deterministic forms of reasoning into the determination of cosmopolitan right. Habermas looks for a space in which the *political urgency* of cosmopolitan solidarity may be given its due and one of the points of contention he has with Kant is that transcendental deductions of the idea of right are insufficiently connected to political processes of deliberation. By embedding individual rights within processes of radical democratic praxis Habermas develops the intuition that rights and democracy cannot be imagined apart from one another. The thought that cosmopolitanism represents the rational will of freely deliberating citizens, and not only the a priori deduction of the philosopher, animates his writings. So, while Kant advocates cosmopolitan politics as a necessary next step in the project of realising the idea of right and the opportunity to opt out of this process or deny the rationality of cosmopolitan justice does not easily cohere with this approach, Habermas sees cosmopolitanism as a desirable political project responding to the inability of the nation-state to realise the freedom of its citizens on the exclusive basis of its own resources. For Habermas, in short, cosmopolitanism furnishes the means by which citizens can, if they so choose, reclaim the scope for agency that contemporary developments have denied. It is a shared project Habermas invites us to join and fashion in our own image and not simply an institutional blueprint projected onto reality.

In the work of Habermas, however, we can scarcely miss the

inclination to depict this particular political and intellectual choice, that of cosmopolitanism, as the choice that is in accord with the law of nature. Against a seemingly intransigent faith in the nation-state, Habermas presents cosmopolitanism as the *logical culmination* of the principles of right on which enlightenment was founded (Habermas 2006: 133). The underlying argument is that the universal principles of right and law, though once swamped by the particularistic self-assertion of one nation against another, are 'best suited to the identity of world citizens, not to that of citizens of a particular state that has to maintain itself against other states'. For Habermas, there is a sense in which the rational necessity of cosmopolitanism is not up for discussion and a democratic community cannot opt out of the project of realising constitutional principles at the national, transnational and global levels. The sense of a Law of Nature asserting itself behind our backs may account for Habermas's insistence that cosmopolitanism is reconcilable with constitutional patriotism and must be institutionalised notwithstanding the problems of political hierarchy and democratic legitimacy this raises.[4] To my mind, this form of reasoning not only irons over the creases of the modern state; it also downplays the difficulties of cosmopolitan judgement in a world which, to say the least, is only partially cosmopolitan.

4

COSMOPOLITANISM AND
INTERNATIONAL LAW[1]

From the 'law of peoples' to the
'constitutionalisation of international law'

This chapter focuses on the role of international law within the 'cosmopolitan condition'. It addresses the *juridical* approach to cosmopolitan thinking taken by Rawls and Habermas and how this differs from those who advocate 'cosmopolitan democracy' or 'global civil society'. I shall argue that whilst there are good reasons for not embracing the perspectives of cosmopolitan democracy and global civil society, something is lost in the process of juridification. The idea of the 'Law of Peoples' put forward by John Rawls sets the scene for cosmopolitan thinking about international law in a way that is correctly described as 'liberal' but it also has some non-cosmopolitan and worrying implications. The case for the 'constitutionalisation of international law' embraced by Habermas creatively builds on his theory of constitutional patriotism at the national and transnational levels. He successfully, to my mind, addresses the defects of Rawls's Law of Peoples but in a manner that raises difficult questions about the status of international law and its relation both to the violence of the state and to the power of the people.

Whilst the meaning of the constitutionalisation of international law is not entirely clear, I argue that it threatens to turn the principles of international law into the foundation of a 'cosmopolitanised' natural law theory and restrict the role of political judgement to a transitional and subordinate moment.

COSMOPOLITAN DEMOCRACY AND GLOBAL CIVIL SOCIETY

Advocates of cosmopolitan democracy (Archibugi 1998, 2000; Held 1995b, 2004) argue that cosmopolitan democracy is distinct from other projects for world government in its attempt to 'create institutions that enable the voice of individuals to be heard in global affairs irrespective of their resonance at home' (Archibugi 2004a: 144). They propose not only the reform of the UN, the WTO and other global bodies but a 'parallel series of democratic institutions' including an assembly of representatives whom the people can elect through international political parties. The task they have undertaken, which I shall not discuss here in any detail, is a difficult one: it is how to conceive of cosmopolitan democracy given that the existing structures of international organisations such as the United Nations or the WTO appear antithetical to democratic norms and given that at the international level the obstacles in the way of establishing democratic norms of representation, administration, enforcement and legitimation are themselves dauntingly high. Nonetheless, there has been much creative thinking about how to establish a cosmopolitan party system and deliberative assembly; how to implement democratic decisions and channel deliberative power into concrete policy initiatives; how to ensure individual state actors comply with cosmopolitan legislation; and how to encourage people to identify with cosmopolitan institutions, accept their decisions and respect other members as free and equal citizens. There has emerged widespread consensus among cosmopolitan writers in favour of reform of the UN and other international institutions, the construction of new institutions of democratic governance and more robust forms of legitimation, either direct or indirect, from global public opinion.

While proposals for democratic reform of and innovation in international institutions are to be treated on their merits, theories of 'cosmopolitan democracy' may be more difficult to sustain. They become especially problematic if they have resonances of establishing a democratic republic writ large – a world state akin to political states at the national level. This way of thinking comes up against the empirical objection that 'the political constitution of a world society lacks the character of a state as a whole' (Habermas 2006: 136) and the normative objection, prefigured by Kant, that a world state is in any case the wrong model for thinking about cosmopolitan order. If we expect the same standards of democratic legitimation as those we demand of republican government, not only might we have to prepare for perpetual disappointment but also for the de-legitimisation of international laws and institutions. Habermas goes further and argues that the concept of 'cosmopolitan democracy' may be self-contradictory in that the all-inclusive character of cosmopolitan institutions excludes democracy in principle:

> Any political community that wants to understand itself as a democracy must at least distinguish between members and non-members. The self-referential concept of collective self-determination demarcates a logical space for democratically united citizens who are members of a particular community. Even if such a community is grounded in the universalistic principles of a democratic constitutional state, it still forms a collective identity in the sense that it interprets and realises these principles in light of its own history and in the context of its own particular form of life. This ethical-political self-understanding of citizens of a particular democratic life is missing in the inclusive community of world citizens.
>
> (Habermas 2001a: 107)

The case Habermas advances is that democratic legitimacy is not possible in a political body that embraces everyone and provides no particular foundation for collective identity or civic solidarity, and that it is not necessary, or as necessary as in nation-states, because international institutions perform limited functions (such as securing peace, promoting human rights and protecting individual rights) and impose only negative duties (no wars of aggression, no violations of human rights, no crimes against humanity). However, we cannot avoid the question theorists of cosmopolitan democracy raise: what is left of democracy at the supra-national level.

Advocates of global civil society look to civil society as a source of de-centred, democratic authority, based on horizontal networks of interconnected 'nodes', capable of co-ordinating action by means of information and communication technology independently both of state and market (Walzer 1995; Castells 2000; Rosenau 2002). Global civil society encompasses transnational non-governmental organisations, social movements and other formal and informal associations that contribute to the growing emphasis on human rights and social justice in the international arena as well as to the implementation of international legislation in domestic jurisdictions. Examples might include the crucial role global civil society played in the Ottawa Convention on Banning Landmines, in the events leading up to the arrest of Pinochet or in the formation of the International Criminal Court (Kaldor 2003). The strength of this perspective lies in its recognition that transnational advocacy networks can play a leading role in bringing issues of public concern to the top of the international agenda and influencing otherwise resistant representative and executive bodies. Civil society arguments provide for the crucial role of publicity, the public uses of reason and the public sphere in world society and for the formal and informal influencing of civil society on legal and decision-making processes (Lara 2007).

Yet the problems of global civil society theory are no less than those of cosmopolitan democracy. Civil society associations arise out of the same political economy as other international institutions, they are subject to the same pressures of co-optation by powerful interests, and their own policy making structures are often just as remote from the deliberations of any representative body (Lupel 2004). In Europe the development of a transnational civil society *in isolation from representative institutions* might even enhance the feeling of detachment of European citizens, since participation in transnational civil society presupposes a range of cognitive skills and social opportunities that may be limited to relatively few citizens within each nation-state. At the national level civil society is a middle term between the private lives of citizens and the political state and it becomes incoherent or positively unsafe when afforded supreme status in its own right. Habermas argues that we have to dispel the *romanticism of civil society* that sees it as an alternative to the representative institutions of modernity. At the global level, where there is no international state in the strict sense of the term, civil society cannot substitute for it. Civil society is not a singular 'subject' with its own undivided will and should not be presented as such (Fine 1997).[2]

If cosmopolitan democracy is too much like a world state and global civil society too little, a 'third way' for the cosmopolitan to take is to look to the development of a form of cosmopolitan law, backed by coercive capacities, to regulate relations between states, protect the basic rights of citizens and impose itself on sovereign legislators as an external constraint. This strategy fits well with a Lockeian form of natural law theory that presents us with an image either of a benevolent grouping of powerful, well-ordered states acting in the best interests of all individual rights-bearers or of a constitutional order legislating, adjudicating and enforcing the rights of subjects. In this third way, questions of democratic legitimacy, civil society initiative and the influence of public opinion are self-consciously downplayed.

JOHN RAWLS AND THE LAW OF PEOPLES

In *The Law of Peoples* Rawls makes the case that 'a constitutional regime must establish an effective Law of Peoples in order to realise fully the freedom of its citizens' (Rawls 1999: 10). The principles he outlines for the Law of Peoples are for the most part philosophical re-formulations of well-established principles of international law. They emphasise the independence and self-determination of peoples, respect for treaties and other agreements between peoples, non-intervention in the internal affairs of other peoples, and norms regulating the conduct of war between peoples. In line with recent directions in international law they also advance more distinctively cosmopolitan themes: peoples are bound to honour human rights, the principle of non-intervention may be suspended in the case of major human rights abuses, and the principles of international law provide the frame of reference for the effective authority of international organisations such as the United Nations or World Trade Organisation.

Rawls denies that the Law of Peoples is a cosmopolitan project.

However, this denial is related to his definition of cosmopolitanism as a commitment to the *social well-being* of all global citizens and to *global distributive justice* (Rawls 1999: 119–20) and to his own refusal in the Law of Peoples to pursue the claim he raises in the context of domestic justice, namely that large social and economic inequalities between parties may generate serious inequalities in political power (Pogge 2001). In fact, the exclusion of social questions from the Law of Peoples does not substantially distinguish Rawls from Kant, or even from Habermas, given his admission that a weak democratic legitimation of the UN 'will suffice for the activity of the world organisation only if the latter restricts itself to the most elementary tasks of securing peace and human rights on a global scale' (Habermas 2006: 174). In any case, a cosmopolitan accent is audible in Rawls's commitment to the legal regulation of relations between peoples, to the legal authority of supranational organisations and to a package of universal human rights (Brown 2002: 178).

And yet there is a certain truth to Rawls's self-assessment. He does show himself to be at least 'half-hearted' in his cosmopolitan enthusiasm. First, he retains the classical notion of bounded political peoples as the basic unit of the Law of Peoples. It is striking, for instance, that in so far as Rawls offers any *argument* in defence of human rights, he mirrors contemporary practice by appealing to 'peace and security' considerations. Rights-violating states are 'aggressive and dangerous', he states, and 'all peoples are safer and more secure if such states change or are forced to change their ways' (Rawls 1999: 81). This defence of human rights remains hostage to the empirical criticism that rights-violating states may not necessarily pose a serious threat to international security and to the moral criticism that rights should be defended irrespective of their functional value in preserving global security (Beitz 2000: 685). The principle of cosmopolitan law, by contrast, starts from the proposition that all persons of the globe are in principle rights-bearing citizens and that world society is not regulated *solely* around the rights and obligations of peoples. For all individuals to enjoy their status as rights-bearing citizens, mechanisms must exist for their human rights to be legally guaranteed beyond the unit of peoples. Multiple strategies for realising world citizenship of this sort might include, for example, avenues for citizens to raise complaints against their own states (through national, international and regional courts), coordinated forms of international pressure on rights-violating states, the establishment of legal precedents to prevent large-scale rights abuses and the enhancement of the publicity-generating functions of global civil society.

Second, Rawls maintains that only those peoples which acknowledge and uphold human rights should be recognised as equal members of a society of peoples. He argues that liberal peoples, by virtue of their commitment to toleration, should incorporate within the society of peoples certain *non-liberal* regimes as 'equal participating members in good standing of the Society of Peoples' in so far as they are sufficiently 'reasonable' (Rawls 1999: 59). He describes a hypothetical 'decent people' (*sic*) as one that does not have aggressive international aims, is regulated around an idea of justice, consults its citizens about the direction of law and policy, and respects certain basic human rights. It maintains some freedom of religion but not necessarily equal freedom of religion, some provisions for political consultation but not necessarily a full range of democratic rights, some respect for women but not necessarily women's equality (Rawls 1999: 71–80). Such a society is not 'liberal' in that it does not respect a full range of equal rights and liberties, does not operate a strict division between state and religion, and does not follow constitutional procedures. Nonetheless, Rawls maintains that such a regime would satisfy a minimal threshold of reasonableness if it respects some basic human rights and accepts the same Law of Peoples as liberal peoples (Rawls 1999: 65–70). For Rawls, this commonality provides a basis on which 'liberal' and 'decent' peoples can co-operate, since both types of societies acknowledge the same Law of Peoples and the same conditions for entering a society of peoples.

The restriction of the society of peoples to 'liberal' peoples and those peoples deemed 'decent' by liberal peoples has echoes of the restrictive principle of membership which once informed the ill-fated League of Nations and does not engage with the actual evolution of world society. It was surpassed by the all-inclusive principle of 'sovereign equality' that now underwrites the UN – even if the price to be paid for this inclusiveness is 'the glaring contradiction between the professed principles of the world body and human rights standards actually practiced by certain member states' (Habermas 2006: 165). The principle embodied in the UN is not to restrict membership of the society of peoples but rather – though very unevenly practised – to make rights-violating states uncomfortable about the gap between their actual practices and the standards they profess by the act of signing up.

Third, Rawls's sixth principle of the Law of Peoples states that peoples are to honour human rights. Human rights are defined as 'a class of rights that play a special role in a reasonable Law of Peoples: they restrict the justifying reasons for war and its conduct, and they specify limits to a regime's internal autonomy' (Rawls 1999: 79). Rawls holds that an external coercive authority can legitimately impose human rights requirements on peoples and speaks of organi-sations charged with correcting violations of human rights through diplomatic pressures, economic sanctions and *in extremis* military intervention (Rawls 1999: 36). He declares that 'outlaw states' can, and under certain circumstances should, become the subject of legitimate intervention when they fail to acknowledge or actively violate the core tenets of the Law of Peoples (Rawls 1999: 81). He does not spell out on what basis a state will be deemed 'outlaw' or by what mechanism this judgement will be authorised.

There is something parochial about an analysis in which Rawls sometimes displays an alarming lack of awareness of the workings of the global economy (Brown 2002: 177). For instance, in his discus-sion of 'burdened societies' he attributes the failure to develop sta-ble and minimally just regimes to a lack of political will and cultural resources and appears to neglect the role of *external factors* in con-tributing to the state of a nation's internal affairs (Rawls 1999: 108). There is also something troubling about the concept of 'outlaw' or 'rogue' states. Partly this is because at the national level the concept of the outlaw state has introduced a fundamentalist outlook into the policies of the US. Nico Krisch argues convincingly that since the mid-1980s the US has developed a category of outlaw states under varying titles – reaching from 'terrorist states' and 'state sponsors of terrorism' to 'rogue states', 'states of concern' and the 'axis of evil'. Initially, these notions mainly served political purposes but since 1996 states designated as 'state-sponsors of terrorism' have legally become second-class states, no longer enjoying the full protection of sovereign states. With the 2002 National Security Strategy outlaw states have become potential objects of pre-emptive self-defence and denied the usual protection in international law of the prohibition on the use of force. Similarly, individuals from 'outlaw states' have been stripped of some of the rights they enjoy under international human rights and humanitarian law – under the title, for instance, of 'unlawful combatants'. The concept of outlaw states has allowed the US to create different categories of states and individuals and to limit the reach of international law to some of them (Krisch 2004).

A critical point at issue here concerns the relation between 'peoples' and 'states'. It seems on the surface that Rawls's preference for the category of 'peoples' over that of 'states' reinforces the cosmopolitan character of his text (Buchanan 2000: 698–700). For Rawls, peoples and states are alike in that they are both bounded political societies whose members share 'common sympathies' and submit to their own law making institutions (Rawls 1999: 23–5). Yet he prefers the concept of 'peoples' to 'states' in order to break from the assumption underpinning classical international law that allows for unrestricted state sovereignty in the pursuit of national interests. Peoples, he argues, are unlike states in that they accept membership of a legal order in which sovereignty is mediated through law and can never be conceived as absolute in terms of external relations with other states or in terms of internal policies towards their own citizens (Rawls 1999: 25–30). This shift in nomenclature sounds promising from a cosmopolitan point of view: it is intended to break from any assumption of absolute or exclusive sovereignty. However, it also collapses a distinction vital to all political thought – between the state and the people over which the state rules. To exclude this or that *people* from the society of peoples on the grounds that its *state* fails to observe basic human rights, opens the gate to all manner of injustice – even if it can be shown that some or many of the people support the state in question. The slippage from condemning a *state* for its human rights abuses to condemning a *people* as unworthy of recognition within the society of peoples is internal to Rawls's theory and sounds an alarmingly anti-cosmopolitan note. It threatens to cross the line between international law and the demonisation of 'outlaw' peoples.

There is also something fixed and restrictive in Rawls's determination of human rights. The limitation of human rights to a 'special class of urgent rights' may be justified if human rights are treated as a ground for intervention but it is unduly restrictive if we wish to advocate a full range of rights and liberties for all global citizens or be in a position to support those who are denied such rights and liberties (McCarthy 1997). It certainly makes it difficult to assimilate ongoing movements towards a more comprehensive doctrine of human rights. We can see such a movement in practice in the emergence of 'democratic rights' (rights to political participation in free and fair elections) as a salient principle of international law (Cassesse 2001: 48–52; Kaldor 2003). This suggests it is unwise to establish once and for all the particular rights that should underpin a Law of Peoples or base membership of the society of peoples on this criterion.[3]

It is characteristic of Rawls to say little about the practical implications or institutional dynamics of this conception of cosmopolitan justice. How serious would a rights violation have to be to justify outside intervention? Which body has the authority to legitimise intervention? What form should intervention take? How is the distinction between 'well-ordered peoples' and 'outlaw states' to be played out in practice? These silences reflect a general feature of Rawls's approach: he sketches the broad outlines of a Law of Peoples but leaves much unsaid about its realisation. Rawls makes a self-conscious decision to stay at the level of ideal theory and leaves it to others to explore how ideal theory can guide reflection and action in actual political circumstances. Ideal theory involves ascertaining the principles that ought to regulate a given association of peoples: 'it should . . . help to clarify the goal of reform and to identify which wrongs are more grievous and hence more urgent to correct' (Rawls 2001: 13). It can inform reflection over issues that emerge where there is non-compliance with principles of justice, including when there is a threat posed by 'outlaw' states, but Rawls acknowledges that the Law of Peoples is incapable of determining action in non-ideal contexts and must be able to draw upon the capacity of political actors to make complex and informed judgements throughout the course of their engagement in political activity (Rawls 1999: 97–8). However, once we begin to think of the actual ways in which this or that people is labelled 'outlaw', the politics of labelling raises all manner of difficult issues. It is notable too that Rawls leaves little space for such judgements to reflect back on the principles they seek to apply. He moves from general principles to particular judgements but seemingly not from particular judgements to the elaboration of general principles.

So while the Law of Peoples lays the groundwork for thinking about the role of international law in international society, there is no avoiding its cosmopolitan limitations. It retains peoples as its basic unit of analysis; it subordinates the protection of human rights to peace and security between states; it restricts membership of the society of peoples to liberal peoples or those approved by liberal peoples; it speaks inexactly of 'outlaw states' and slips into the stigmatisation of whole peoples; it neglects reflective judgement in the determination of the Law of Peoples; and it has little to say about the problems of putting ideal theory into practice. In the face of these limitations I shall turn to Habermas for a more defensible approach and his reformulation of the cosmopolitan condition in terms of what he calls the 'constitutionalisation of international law'.

THE CONSTITUTIONALISATION OF INTERNATIONAL LAW

The idea of the 'constitutionalisation of international law' is drawn from international legal theory as a means of defending the legitimacy of international law despite its expanded scope and increasing distance from the consent of states (Kumm 2004; Rosenau 2002; Teubner 2004). A key indicator of the constitutionalisation of international law is the enhanced authority of the UN and its involvement not only in conflicts *between* states but also in conflicts *within* states – in response to civil wars, the breakdown of government and major human rights abuses or for the promotion of democracy. It reflects an increasing public engagement with international law. Whether a particular action is or is not in accord with international law or the principles of international law, and whether international law has to change to accommodate a particular action, have become the stuff of public debate since 1989 – in contrast with its relative invisibility in the post-1945 period when international law was widely regarded as ineffective or narrowly technocratic in its concerns and citizens were inclined to rely on the resources of domestic legal systems. Today, international law not only claims a 'soft' influence over states to take human rights into account, it demands compliance and declares a duty to obey. Its subject matter has expanded to such an extent that there is no clear nucleus of sovereignty states can invoke against it. Its dependence on state consent and the state's degree of freedom in interpreting and enforcing the law have both significantly diminished. Meanwhile non-state actors such as international courts and tribunals, transnational executives, non-governmental organisations (NGOs) and multinational corporations (MNCs) have emerged as major players in international legal processes.

There are very good reasons for citizens to endorse the constitutional principles of international law, even in opposition to the positive laws of the international community (Kumm 2004). International law can be an asset for the world community as a whole in fostering human rights, protecting welfare, enabling co-operation and building up trust.[4] It can help protect minorities within states and curtail the abuse of power by states. It can further the right of a people to self-government and freedom from domination by other states. It can generalise norms of democratic legitimacy through representative institutions and compensate for the structural deficits of national processes of decision-making when they lead to outcomes that are unacceptable from a more global point of view. The constitutionalisation of international law aims at resolving the split between human rights law and the gross violations of human rights that occur in practice through the formation of 'a world organisation with the power to impose peace and implement human rights' (Habermas 2006: 136). It looks to the construction of a rule of law in the international arena based on the principles of equal sovereignty, human rights and the authority of international law itself. It involves extending the scope of international law, increasing its range of authority and distancing it from the immediate consent of states. It declares that the norms of international law now function as a higher law vis-à-vis that of states; that they include prohibitions on torture, genocide, crimes against humanity, disappearances and other such activities; and that there is an increasing number of rules that obligate all states whether or not they have signed the treaty in question. One of the advantages of thinking in terms of the constitutionalisation of international law is its holistic focus. It encourages us to keep in mind the whole menu of considerations that determine the legitimacy of international law and not pick and choose this or that element (Kumm 2004: 929).[5]

Habermas presents the constitutionalisation of international law as an alternative to 'realist' and 'ethical' conceptions of the primacy of power over law, the former rooted in classical international law and the latter in the hegemonic unilateralism of the US. He sees constitutionalisation as the condition of the transformation of international law from an instrument of power into 'the crucible in which quasi-natural power relations could be dissolved' (Habermas 2006: 149). In the framework of the nation-state, Habermas writes, 'the fusion of command and law initially means that law is at the service of power or law is the means by which power is organised ... Constitutionalisation *reverses* the initial situation in which law serves as an instrument of power' (Habermas 2006: 130–2, my italic). Reversal means that rather than law serving as an instrument of power, power serves as an instrument of law. In identifying the 'cosmopolitan condition' with the constitutionalisation of international law, Habermas manifestly draws on his earlier conception of constitutional patriotism. He argues that it is the *constitution* of the nation-state, not the state itself, which provides the appropriate model for the transition from classical to cosmopolitan international law. The opposition Habermas discerns between the universal principles of the constitution and the power of the nation-state is heightened at the international level so that the constitution is dissociated altogether from the formation of an international state. Whilst in the national context the political state and constitution are fused in one and the same institution, in the international arena one finds a legal order without a state, the rule of law without democratic legislation. The analogy is more with pre-modern forms of law not yet integrated into a single state system. Habermas goes back to natural law to be able to think forward. He demonstrates the asymmetry between the evolution of the nation-state and that of cosmopolitan order by reference to existing structures of international law, perceived as capable of performing their basic functions of securing peace and promoting human rights without having to assume a state-like character. As with every law, international laws can never be valid simply because they exist. There is always the possibility of conflict between what they are and what they ought to be. The constitutional principles of international law provide for Habermas a rational foundation for criticism and reform of positive international laws. What we see here is an adaptation of the theory of constitutional patriotism to the arena of world society.

A key political question Habermas faces is whether the reformulation of the cosmopolitan project in terms of the constitutionalisation of international law is doomed to failure because of American imperial power. He forestalls pessimism by arguing that the American turn to hegemonic unilateralism represents a recent, and hopefully temporary, reversal of its more enduring commitment to an internationalist strategy as well as a neglect of its own long-term rational interest in 'binding emerging major powers to the rules of a politically constituted international community' (Habermas 2006: 150).[6] More problematic for Habermas is the relation of the constitutionalisation of international law to his own theory of the co-originality of rights and democracy: how is one to defend this legal conception of a cosmopolitan world order from the charge that it lacks democratic legitimacy? Habermas is reluctant to go all the way with the liberal tradition of natural law, 'from Locke to Dworkin', that draws its resources exclusively from the natural order of things. He does not wish to sever supranational constitutions altogether from the channels of democratic legitimation institutionalised within the nation-state and to a lesser degree within transnational federations. He sees various connections remaining intact: the normative substance of supranational constitutions rest on rights, legal principles and criminal codes tried and tested within democratic constitutions; supranational constitutions receive indirect backing from democratic processes that are only institutionalised in nation-states; global communication in an informal public sphere confers a supplementary level of democratic legitimacy on the decisions of the world organisation even without institutionalised paths for translating influence into political power. Nonetheless, Habermas recognises that the constitutionalisation of international law does *not* satisfy republican standards of democratic legitimation and justifies this deficit on the ground that international law is in its very nature distinct from the law of a nation-state and performs relatively limited functions compared with political states. His acknowledgement that international law can never have the same level of democratic legitimacy as republican government raises difficult questions not just about the validity of Habermas's 'co-originality' thesis but about the political costs that might be involved in constitutionalising international law. These costs cannot be spirited away by rationalising what already exists.

The idea of 'the constitutionalisation of international law' is based on the recognition that international law imposes restraints on the exercise of hegemony by powerful states. The rules of international law limit their freedom of action; the stability it demands prevents any rapid reshaping of international norms; the formal egalitarianism it imposes makes it difficult for hegemonic powers to apply rules to others which it does not apply to itself. It is also based on the recognition that great powers may respond to these restraints with a variety of strategies: they may instrumentalise existing international law to suit their own interests; they may reshape the concepts and rules of international law, say, to exempt themselves from its provisions or provide more space for them to intervene in the affairs of other states; they may create zones of exclusion where the norms of international law have no purchase (as in Guantanamo Bay); they may substitute domestic law over which they retain control for the less certain authority of international law; or they may withdraw altogether from international law and simply bring their military superiority to bear. However, big powers may also have an interest in supporting international law for reasons to do with global regulation (it sets rules), pacification (it reduces resistance), stabilisation (it preserves the current order) and legitimation (it justifies power). To be sure, all such strategies involve trade-offs but the normative project of constitutionalising international law is not necessarily at odds with the realities of state power or capitalist interest. The associations and parties of global civil society may also develop instrumental strategies in relation to international law but they too have an interest in its capacities to uphold human rights and inhibit the abuse of power by states.

THE LIMITS OF CONSTITUTIONALISATION

The theory of the constitutionalisation of international law offers an intellectually stimulating and politically rich way of re-interpreting the cosmopolitan condition. Let us consider more critically, however, this juridical turn. The notion that international law *already* has a constitution, either written in the UN Charter or unwritten, would blind us to the political instrumentalisation of existing international law. Jean Cohen puts the matter plainly: the idea that the power of the state has already been reduced to the status of servant of international law runs the real risk of 'dressing up strategic power-plays . . . in a universalistic garb' (Cohen 2004: 10).

In addition, there may be deeper conceptual problems in the very idea of the constitutionalisation of international law. In her essay on 'What is authority?' Hannah Arendt makes reference to Montesquieu's judicial branch of government whose power he called 'somehow nil' and which nevertheless constitutes the highest authority in constitutional governments. It is, as Mommsen put it, 'more than advice and less than command, an advice which one may not safely ignore' (Arendt 1977a: 122–3). It builds on the notion of authority established in the tradition of natural law, in which the source of authority transcends power and those in power. In the past this notion of authority relied on religious trust in a sacred beginning and traditional and unquestioned standard of behaviour. Today, Arendt comments, 'to live in a world with neither authority nor the concomitant awareness that the source of authority transcends power . . . means to be confronted anew . . . by the elementary problems of human living together' (Arendt 1977a: 141). The analogy is not exact but the constitutionalisation of international law bears resemblance to the idea of a branch of government whose power is nil but which still represents the highest authority in world society. We do not have to endorse an 'ontology of power' (an ideology which roots the incessant drive for power in human nature and reduces all questions of justice to those of power) to recognise that the authority of international law in world society can no longer be based on such traditional grounds. We may set our sight on the establishment of an international law no longer distorted by power, whose authority transcends power, but whether power is identified with the violence of the state or with the deliberations of a democratic political community, international law may prove an insufficiently effective regulator in the face of the intransigence of the one and the collective creativity of the other.[7]

The relation between law and politics needs to be conceptualised outside the dichotomy of either law serving power or power serving law. On the one hand, law rarely just serves power and if it does it ceases to be law; it is rather a form of power, a mediation of power, and it implies some level of inhibition on power. On the other hand, power never just serves law; law is part of society and contains within itself the power relations that traverse society; power is integral to law. In its attempt to find remedies for crimes against humanity, genocide, ethnic cleansing and other forms of mass murder, terror, torture and rape, I do not think cosmopolitan social theory should endorse the myth of a wholly legalised international order, a constitutionalised international law, still to come. The problem is not just one of treating the constitutionalisation of international law as if it were already established, when it is in fact highly contested and only in its infancy (Cohen 2004: 11), but one of conceptualising the cosmopolitan condition in these exclusively juridical terms.

Habermas writes of the transition from classical international law to cosmopolitan law, that is, from an international law based on the sovereignty of states to a cosmopolitan law based on the rights of citizens. We need to be careful, however, in how we handle this concept of transition, which can be misleading for a number of reasons. First, the so-called Westphalian system of international relations disappeared long ago. The universalism of the natural law framework that governed this system was restricted in practice to European states, offered little obstacle to the justification of colonialism and imposed prohibitions on war that were at best weakly applied. Second, the classical international law that evolved in the course of the twentieth century, and especially after 1945, was based on the principle of sovereign equality for all member states, imposed a universal norm of non-aggression and non-intervention on all states and rejected all forms of colonialism. Third, internal sovereignty was never an absolute claim to unlimited power unrestrained by law – even in its most Hobbesian moments. It indicated for nation-states the establishment of a public authority that ruled through law and in its more developed versions through a separation of powers in which the idea of popular sovereignty was given institutional expression. Fourth, external sovereignty was never a claim to be able to wage war at will. It indicated mutual recognition among a plurality of autonomous political communities according to a growing body of international law whose basic principle was that agreements between states had to be respected. Nor was external sovereignty an exclusive claim for non-interference in a state's internal affairs since it always depended on the state's ability to act as a public authority. Fifth, sovereignty in general expresses a particular form of political community and a particular relation of the rulers to the ruled. It is, however, not a fixed form and among the changes it has undergone we find the domestic constitutionalisation of civil and political rights and the international elaboration of human rights.

Even Schmitt recognised that in the past, the 'Westphalian' order was based on shared political norms involving mutual recognition and institutionalised co-operation between states:

> Such an order was not a lawless chaos of egoistic wills to power . . . these egoistic power structures existed side-by-side in the same space of one European order, wherein they mutually recognised each other as sovereigns. Each was the equal of the other, because each constituted a moment of the system of equilibrium.
>
> (Schmitt 2003: 167)

Regarding the future, what is at stake is not the 'end' of sovereignty or its displacement by human rights but rather a process of democratisation. While for Kant classical international law (between states) and cosmopolitan law (between subjects and across states) are supposed to co-exist, for Habermas classical international law and cosmopolitan law appear as discrete historical stages. Kant spoke of the co-existence of classical international law and cosmopolitan law, rather than a transition from one to the other. He may have had a good point. It certainly makes little sense to speak of the death of sovereignty in the context of the constitutionalisation of international law, for the end of sovereignty can only indicate a regression from international law in favour of some other principle of domination.

This is not to reject the idea of transition from classical to cosmopolitan international law, but it is to take issue with the idealisation of international law in a new cosmopolitan cloth. My contention is that we should resist the temptation to present the principles of international law as if they were the natural law of the cosmopolis against which all other positive laws must be measured or to attribute the political abuse of international law simply to the incompleteness of the transition. The only problem from this perspective is, as Jean Cohen points out, 'the restricted reach of global remedies: the ICJ lacks compulsory jurisdiction, the ICC lacks a definition for the crime of aggression, the Security Council is legally unrestrained . . . When these restrictions are overcome, law will be able to control politics' (Cohen 2004: 11). Many cosmopolitans look forward to a time to come when the UN will have its own army and its own legal mechanisms for deciding when to use it as the *sine qua non* of subordinating power to international law (Habermas and Derrida 2003a). We may share the aspiration to develop more robust forms of international and cosmopolitan law, but as I shall argue in the next chapter, we should resist the temptation to overburden law by exaggerating its attractiveness and capabilities (Hirsh 2005). We have to leave space for the political field of judgement. The task, as I see it, is not so much to constitutionalise international law but to attach it more firmly to a cosmopolitan politics.

5

COSMOPOLITANISM AND HUMANITARIAN MILITARY INTERVENTION

War, peace and human rights

This chapter addresses an uneasy question: the relation between cosmopolitanism and humanitarian military intervention.[1] The re-emergence of cosmopolitanism as a flourishing intellectual project has coincided with what Michael Ignatieff describes as a 'new tide of interventionist internationalism', whereby Western nations have become embroiled in various efforts to 'put the world to rights' (Ignatieff, 1999: 3). Perhaps the most contentious element of this interventionism has been the willingness to use military force for humanitarian ends. Prominent examples of allegedly humanitarian military interventions include US intervention, sanctioned by the United Nations, in Somalia between 1992 and 1994 and NATO's air campaign, not officially sanctioned by the United Nations, in Kosovo and Serbia in 1999. Prior to the 1990s debate was provoked on this issue by India's intervention into Bangladesh in 1971, Vietnam's intervention into Cambodia in 1978–9 and Tanzania's intervention into Uganda in 1979 (Wheeler 2000). In the first half of the 1990s the Security Council of the UN authorised peace-keeping interventions in eight instances and military interventions in a further five. Today, there is extensive debate over the foibles and follies of the US/UK invasion of Iraq, the refusal of the UN to grant legitimacy to the military exercise and retrospective attempts to justify the invasion in humanitarian terms (McGoldrick 2004).

The practice of humanitarian military intervention goes to the heart of cosmopolitan aims to defend human rights and it raises searching questions about whether and how individuals can be safeguarded against the murderous actions of their own governments. Support for humanitarian military intervention is premised on the widespread feeling that the exercise of military force has been both possible and urgently needed to stop grave humanitarian crimes. It is also provoked by the consequences that have ensued from the failure of the international community to act effectively in the face of genocide in Rwanda in 1994 (Wheeler, 2000: 208–41) and ethnic cleansing in Bosnia throughout the 1990s (Bobbitt, 2002: 414–67). Today some observers say that crimes against humanity and possibly genocide are occurring among the African populations of Darfur and Zimbabwe and yet there has be till now little evidence that the international community is prepared to intervene with any significant show of military force (Reeves 2005).

The chapter is also triggered by the serious criticisms coming from both ends of the political spectrum on the damage humanitarian military intervention has done to the whole cosmopolitan project. Consider, for example, the comments of mainly leftist critics of cosmopolitanism in an interesting collection *Debating Cosmopolitics* (Archibugi 2004b). The sociologist Geoffrey Hawthorne re-affirms the continuing relevance of state formation in parts of the world where states are barely able to exercise control over their own territory or ensure the security of their own citizens. For Hawthorne, the key political question concerns how failed and failing states are to be re-formed. His article of faith is that states cannot be repaired through military interventions and he is particularly sceptical of liberals who claim the right to use force in the name of humanity. David Chandler declares that the NATO bombing of Yugoslavia was a clear breach of international law and more generally that cosmopolitan arguments which endorse the limitation of sovereignty for some states in effect grant the right to intervene at will to others. He maintains that the new interventionism is a throwback to a time when state sovereignty was the privilege of the few and powerful states granted themselves the right to use force against the less powerful. According to Chandler, cosmopolitanism should be read as an attack on the principle of sovereign equality introduced after 1945. Similarly, Tim Brennan identifies cosmopolitanism with *Pax Americana* dressed up in the cloth of international law. He is dismissive of cosmopolitan concerns over crimes against humanity, referring to them as 'fear-mongering cameos of "tribal" blood-letting in barbaric backlands', and interprets the cosmopolitan attack on national sovereignty as an attack on the capacity of 'indigenous peoples to draw a boundary between what is theirs and what lies beyond' (Archibugi 2004a: 46). Peter Gowan argues that the formation of a supra-state authority, far from exercising jurisdiction over the US, is destined to become its lightly disguised instrument. For Gowan, the cosmopolitan dream of uniting humanity on the basis of a global citizenry and universal human rights is a self-deception, since no scheme for universal harmony can work which fails to confront the social relations of actually existing capitalism.

The gap between facts and norms leads some critics to conclude that the cosmopolitan outlook is either hopelessly naive or wilfully cynical (Zolo 2002; Chomsky 1999). Most of these writers reserve their severest criticism for the doctrine that there can be a right of intervention even without the formal authorisation of the UN. They see the appeal to 'global justice' as an umbrella under which an attack on international law is being launched by big powers and see cosmopolitanism as, naively or wilfully, justifying an imperial international order. Jacques Rancière argues that under a cosmopolitan register the rights of man have become the rights of victims: 'of those unable to enact any rights or even any claim in their name, so that eventually their rights had to be upheld by others, at the cost of shattering the edifice of international law, in the name of a new right of humanitarian interference' (Rancière 2006). He concludes that the rights of man or human rights (he equates the two) have been boiled down to a right of invasion, a right of war, which is in effect no right at all. He argues that since the invasion of Iraq the idea of humanitarian military intervention has become so deeply imbricated in a new imperialism as to drag the larger cosmopolitan project down with it.

These arguments are compelling but to my mind they leave

unanswered the question that gives rise to cosmopolitan think-ing in the first place. If people are hunted out of their homes and threatened with ethnic slaughter, should there not be humanitarian military intervention if this is feasible? Is there not a responsibility attached to power not to remain inactive in the face of gross inhu-manity? Why should our sense of responsibility stop at national boundaries? What does the slogan 'never again' mean if it excludes in principle military interventions designed to stop genocides? Should we really be nostalgic about the classical system of interna-tional law whose core principle was that of non-intervention under all circumstances, including the murderous abuse by the state of its own subjects, and whose practice allowed the US and the USSR to do as they willed in their own 'backyards'? Is there not a sense of self-serving cant in the claims of rulers that international action over their mistreatment of minorities is unwarranted interference in their internal affairs? Critics of cosmopolitanism must engage with the problem to which cosmopolitanism is a response: never again to be indifferent to the deliberate mass destruction of human lives simply because the perpetrators are ordained by a sovereign nation-state or because the victims are foreigners. In a world which now has experience of totalitarian terror and annihilation, the cosmopolitan imagination refuses to rule out the need for humanitarian military intervention. Instead, it seeks to establish a firm ethical and legal basis on which to decide under what circumstances humanitarian military intervention might be justified, through what institutions such interventions are to be authorised and by what means such interventions are to be conducted.

When people are subjected to ethnic cleansing, crimes against humanity or genocide at the hands of the authorities that rule them, the cosmopolitan intuition is that there must be a form of ethical life beyond that of their own state to which they have a right to appeal and from which they can have a realistic expectation of support. From this perspective humanitarian military intervention appears as one element in the construction of a sense of universal responsibil-ity. While it does not address the big issues concerning the origins of totalitarian tendencies in our own world, the new cosmopolitanism enjoins us to think hard about the conditions of its legitimacy. The results are as interesting for what they reveal about the emerging cosmopolitan paradigm as for what they offer to ongoing debates about military intervention.

DEALING WITH AMBIVALENCE

One of the main characteristics of cosmopolitanism in relation to humanitarian military intervention is equivocation in the face of competing pressures. On the one hand, cosmopolitan principles of human rights and global governance lend support to humanitarian military intervention if it is deemed necessary in order to protect the basic human rights of the most vulnerable. Humanitarian military intervention appears as an extension of the precedent set at Nuremberg: if evidence of crimes against humanity can serve as a basis for legal prosecution after the event, then it can also serve as a basis for military intervention to prevent or stop the crimes themselves. If 'universal responsibility' is to mean anything, it is the responsibility of those who have the power not to stand idly by when crimes against humanity are being committed and it is within their capacities to end them. On the other hand, cosmopolitanism is historically associated with the critique of militarism, the search for alternatives to war and the ideal of 'perpetual peace'. Not for nothing did Kant call the contract he envisaged between nation-states *foedus pacificum* – the peace-making pact. The normative philosophy of Kantian cosmopolitanism endorses the categorical imperative to put an end to war. The new cosmopolitanism is suspicious of a humanitarian rhetoric that conceals the exercise of dominance on the part of powerful states and there are many who fear that the legitimisation of violence in terms of human rights can only delay the construction of a genuine universal human rights culture (Booth 2001: 314). Their credo is that the governance of international affairs through cosmopolitan norms requires non-violent processes of communicative interaction (Young 2007). The ambivalence of cosmopolitanism manifests itself in the fact that individuals who share similar cosmopolitan principles can and do come to opposite conclusions with regard both to the principle of humanitarian military interventions and its application to particular situations. The question the new cosmopolitanism faces is how to deal with ambivalence without denying either side of it and without being paralysed by it.

I shall consider what I take to be the prevailing strategy of the new cosmopolitanism: it is to specify in precise terms the criteria of justification, authorisation and military conduct which humanitarian military intervention must meet if it is to be deemed legitimate. I consider this to be a necessary and productive strategy but one that can never do the work that is expected of it. The argument runs roughly as follows.

First, military action becomes justifiable only in the context of 'supreme humanitarian emergencies'. We have to distinguish between 'the ordinary routine abuse of human rights that tragically occurs on a daily basis and those extraordinary acts of killing and brutality that belong to the category of "crimes against humanity"' (Wheeler 2000: 34). In the latter category Nicholas Wheeler includes state-sponsored mass murder and mass population expulsions by force and genocide (Wheeler 2000: 34). Whilst no cosmopolitan writer claims to provide an unambiguous distinction between acceptable and unacceptable humanitarian crimes, most trade on the idea of crimes which 'shock the conscience of humanity' (Walzer 2000: 107). Daniele Archibugi, for example, makes the dubious contention that

> whilst debate continues to rage over the acceptability of practices such as stoning adulterous wives . . . no one would dream of urging military intervention to foreign countries to ban these practices . . . it is quite plain and straightforward that military humanitarian intervention is necessary when and only when blatant collective violations of human rights are being perpetrated.
> (Archibugi 2004c: 6)

According to Richard Falk, the moral and legal requirements for intervention are satisfied only if 'the governing process has collapsed or is widely perceived as engaged in massive and gross violations of human rights amounting to "crimes against humanity", especially if there is a genocidal element present' (Falk 1998: 96).

The universal emphasis on human rights violations to be found in the literature may be misplaced in that the only grounds for humanitarian military intervention actually given are not to do with violation of human rights as such but with the commission of serious crimes under international criminal law. Even so, military action is still only justified as *a means of last resort*, with much of the debate over the Kosovo intervention revolving around whether or not the intervening powers were seriously committed to finding a diplomatic solution (Chomsky 1999: 22–3; Falk, 1999: 855). There must be some sort of *proportionality threshold* in the sense that military action has a reasonable chance of not causing more harm than it resolves (Wheeler 2000: 36–7; Archibugi 2004c: 11–13). And pre-emptive intervention is valid only if intervening parties are convinced that mass killings are imminent and that it makes no sense to wait for them to start (Wheeler 2000: 34–5). In Rwanda it is argued that speedy action *before* the genocide unfolded was possible, given that there had been clear and urgent warnings to the international community (Barnett 2003: 175).

Second, it is an important cosmopolitan principle that humanitarian military interventions must be given legal authorisation at the global level. States should not be able simply to appeal to their own interpretation of cosmopolitan principles to justify military interventions without being constrained by legal procedures for determining whether or not such an appeal is appropriate. This idea is central to the Habermasian rebuttal of the 'Schmittian' complaint that humanitarian military intervention constitutes a dangerous moralisation of warfare:

> the establishment of the desired situation of world citizenship would not mean that violations of basic human rights are evaluated and fought off in an unmediated way according to philosophical *moral* standards, but instead are prosecuted as criminal acts within a state-ordained legal order.
>
> (Habermas 1999a: 269)

Humanitarian military interventions are conceived not so much as a species of war but rather as *police actions* designed to enforce cosmopolitan laws (Kaldor 2003: 134). One can even imagine with Daniele Archibugi the establishment of a world court to act as a deliberative body or to determine publicly whether humanitarian crimes are serious enough to merit military intervention (Archibugi 2004c: 10). In addition, members of global civil society and regionally active civil society groups, aided by the world press, may have a significant role in forming public opinion and influencing the decision to intervene and this can be taken to the point of their being granted some kind of formal institutional representation at the global level (Archibugi 2004c: 12; Kaldor 2001: 119–24). The aim in all cases is to maximise the role that genuine humanitarian concerns play in deliberation leading up to any decision over the use of force and to minimise the possibility of humanitarian concerns acting as a cover for other interests.

Third, cosmopolitan criteria must be established concerning the *conduct* of humanitarian military intervention. These include restrictions on military conduct familiar from international law: intervening states must not put innocent persons at risk in order to protect the lives of their own forces and the rights of enemy soldiers and non-combatants must be respected. Restrictions should be placed on the bombing of 'dual-function' facilities that have both military and civilian functions and are 'vital to the minimal functioning of the society', such as the infrastructure guaranteeing the provision of electricity, clean water, medical care and basic sanitation (Shue 2003: 108–9). In the face of the threat of 'total war' it is imperative to preserve 'some minimal form of human society to continue during the war' (Shue 2003: 102). Rawls puts it simply: 'well-ordered peoples must respect, so far as possible, the human rights of the members of the other side, both civilians and soldiers' (Rawls 1999: 96). The most distinctive contribution of cosmopolitanism lies in its account of changes in military strategy necessary if militaries are to respond to violations of humanitarian law in a humanitarian way. There is a commitment to training, equipping and motivating military forces to engage in civil rescue operations, humanitarian missions and reconstruction. 'Cosmopolitan-minded militaries' differ from conventional state-based militaries: 'unlike war-fighting, in which the aim is to maximise casualties on the other side and to minimise casualties on your own side . . . cosmopolitan law-enforcement has to minimise casualties on all sides' (Kaldor 2001: 129–30). The strategic imperative of cosmopolitan militaries is not primarily to win wars or overpower an enemy, but to see military victory as a means of securing the end of state-organised atrocities: 'Whereas the soldier, as the legitimate bearer of arms, had to be prepared to die for his country, the international soldier/policeman risks his or her life for humanity' (Kaldor 2001: 131). Military strategies must be designed to 'protect citizens and stabilise war situations so that non-extremist tolerant politics has space to develop' (Kaldor 2003:

134). The more optimistic cosmopolitan may look forward to a time when 'military forces may move . . . to the forefront of the movement concerned with seeing in a more just, equitable and humane world, to become a kind of global social movement for peace and security, or a true "force for good"' (Elliott and Cheeseman 2002: 55). In all cases the central challenge is to carve out a form of military intervention that can respond to the charge that any military response necessarily involves unacceptable destruction of human life and social infrastructure.

When we consider the rigorous criteria of justification, authorisation and military conduct that have to be met if a military intervention is to be legitimated in humanitarian terms, it becomes clear that the new cosmopolitanism intends to strike a balance between its commitment to the protection of human rights, by force if necessary, and its commitment to perpetual peace and the abolition of war. The concern that humanitarian military intervention enables imperial powers to intervene in the internal affairs of less powerful states is allayed by the high hurdles any intervention has to jump to warrant the label of humanitarian. This is as it should be. However, the very height of the hurdles creates its own problems. In the spirit of Rawls, the new cosmopolitanism offers a set of principles which prescribe how military action ought to be carried out in an ideal world in which states are motivated by cosmopolitan norms, international bodies exist to render an authoritative judgement about the need for intervention and military forces are trained and motivated to enforce cosmopolitan laws. Idealisations are injected into every stage of this theory. It describes how military action should be carried out in a more or less cosmopolitan world but says little about what happens in the face of the 'non-ideal' complexities of a world order in which powerful states have interests that conflict with cosmopolitan purposes, human rights law and international criminal law lack reliable enforcement mechanisms, and military forces are tied to the organising principle of the nation-state. When we factor in the 'non-ideal' conditions of the actual world order, its shifting hierarchy of powers and the passions, prejudices and particular interests of political life, the original sense of equivocation is destined to return. For in any particular case an actual 'humanitarian military intervention' is bound to fall short of the high ideals set out within the cosmopolitan framework.

Powerful states or groupings of states undoubtedly pursue geo-strategic interests in conflict with cosmopolitan norms. They not only have the greater capacity to intervene militarily but more influence than weaker states over the interpretation of international law and over the determination of what is and is not a 'supreme humanitarian emergency'. In the face of these considerations, cosmopolitans may focus less on the motives of intervening actors than on the consequences of their military actions. Nicholas Wheeler, for instance, is prepared to endorse distinctively non-humanitarian motivations on the part of intervening states if the interests of the victims are nonetheless met. The complaint that state actors might have ulterior motives for intervention 'is an objection to humanitarian intervention only if the non-humanitarian motives behind an intervention undermine its stated humanitarian purposes' (Wheeler 2000: 39). On the other hand, Richard Falk has argued that we cannot overlook the extent to which 'interventionary claims are exclusively mounted by powerful states that have often in the past put forward self-serving rationalizations for their questionable uses of force to coerce weaker countries with what appears to be an anti-humanitarian net-effect' (Falk 1998: 98). Faced with the coincidence of instrumental and ethical concerns among intervening powers, cosmopolitans may be forced to choose between endorsing humanitarian military intervention despite the motives of intervening powers (e.g. for geo-political advantage or for control of oil resources) or rejecting humanitarian military intervention despite the urgent plight of the victims of terror for fear of the advantages accruing to the powers that intervene.

The principle that humanitarian military interventions should be authorised by an appropriate international decision-making procedure should also address the unsatisfactory character of existing institutional arrangements. According to the Charter, the Security Council has the authority to determine whether or not a particular emergency calls for the use of military intervention to restore international peace and security. No mention is made of military intervention to enforce respect for fundamental human rights, though during the 1990s the Security Council has interpreted threats to international peace and security more widely to include humanitarian crimes under this register (Holzgrefe 2003: 41–3). The Security Council, however, retains the discretion to interpret its mandate as it sees fit and the current arrangement, which allows humanitarian actions to be vetoed by one or more of the permanent members of the Security Council, makes the decision to enforce humanitarian law responsive to the political interests of a minority of powerful states (Archibugi 2004c). Faced with the absence of satisfactory international institutions, cosmopolitans may be forced to choose between endorsing illegal action by a particular state or coalition of states to protect human rights by force or staying loyal to an international legal authority which is incapable of offering an effective regime of rights enforcement but at least contains powerful states within the framework of international law.

Cosmopolitans clearly divide and are divided over this issue. In his discussion of NATO's unauthorised intervention in Kosovo, Jürgen Habermas makes allowances for 'emergency situations' that might entitle democratic states or regional alliances of democratic states to intervene without the formal authority of the United Nations. He reaches this conclusion as a consequence of the tension between legitimacy and effectiveness brought about by the low level of the institutionalisation of cosmopolitan law: 'the dilemma of having to act as though there were already a fully institutionalised global civil society ... does not force us to accept the maxim that victims are to be left at the mercy of thugs' (Habermas 1999a: 271; see also Wheeler 2000: 41–4). Against this, Daniele Archibugi is circumspect about states or regional bodies acting outside existing frameworks of international law. He argues that 'the authority of the United Nations ought to be preferred to unilateral decisions taken by states or state alliances' and that discretion leads right back to a 'state of nature' where states decide on the basis of their own interests when and how to carry out acts of military intervention (Archibugi 2004c: 9). Chomsky puts the case bluntly. In the 'real world' there are only two options: on one side, 'some kind of framework of world order, perhaps the UN Charter, the International Court of Justice, and other existing institutions, or perhaps something better if it can be devised and broadly accepted'; on the other side, 'the powerful do as they wish, expecting to receive the accolades that are the prerogative of power' (Chomsky 1999: 154).

Finally, the obstacles to reforming military forces and strategic cultures to suit the imperatives of cosmopolitan law enforcement are stark. National military forces are often unable and unwilling to conduct themselves in anything like a cosmopolitan fashion. They are trained and equipped for combat, not for rescue operations, and intervening powers are often unwilling to risk their own troops for the sake of saving strangers. Humanitarian missions may be carried out in circumstances where the distinction between combatants and non-combatants is blurred, so that military forces trained to fight clearly recognisable opponents struggle to adapt to demanding new conditions. Humanitarian missions require political skills such as winning the respect of the local populations in targeted regions and working with locally based civil society groups, and existing military forces are frequently unable or unwilling to carry out the basic functional requirements of this political purpose. In these circumstances it is possible reluctantly to endorse military intervention on the grounds that some kind of response is better than none in the face of humanitarian crimes; it is equally possible reluctantly to condemn military intervention because the proposed remedy does not live up to cosmopolitan criteria.

In all cases we are confronted with reluctance against reluctance: a reluctance to endorse a humanitarian military intervention that does not live up to cosmopolitan criteria versus a reluctance to absolve powerful states of their responsibility in the face of humanitarian catastrophes. Once the ideal character of this cosmopolitan approach is brought down to earth, we discover that equivocation returns. This is not a reason to dismiss it. Cosmopolitan theories of military intervention perform important functions: they clarify and systematise our convictions, they provide a framework for making judgements in particular situations; they act as a stimulus for legal and institutional reforms. However, specification of criteria does not resolve ambivalence; it lifts it to another level. The downside of the specification of criteria is the radical indeterminacy present in their application to concrete situations.

There have been various attempts to resolve the problem of radical indeterminacy. Consider, for example, the concept of 'responsibility to protect' which was formulated by the high-profile International Commission on Intervention and State Sovereignty set up by the Canadian government in 2001. It called for a fresh approach that looked at the problem from the victims' point of view and replaced what it saw as the atavistic terminology of sovereignty and human rights with the new language of 'responsibility to protect' (Bellamy

2005). It holds that the primary responsibility to protect lies with the host state. If the host state proves unwilling or unable to fulfil its responsibilities, then secondary responsibility lies with domestic authorities working in partnership with outside agencies. If both these levels fail, then a humanitarian emergency warrants outside intervention. At this level it accepts the view that legal authority for action is vested in the Security Council and that states should always seek its authorisation before using force. If the Security Council is deadlocked, then the potential intervener or interveners should approach the General Assembly. If that fails to produce a result, outside states should intervene if possible through regional alliances. The Commission supported the principle that, should the Security Council fail to fulfil its responsibility to protect because of a veto by one of its permanent members, then other states may take it upon themselves to act. It places on the Security Council two 'just cause thresholds' for intervention (large scale loss of life and ethnic cleansing) and four 'precautionary principles' (right intention, last resort, proportional means and reasonable prospects of success).

The report expressed a growing consensus in international law for the desirability of intervention in supreme humanitarian emergencies when authorised by the Security Council and perhaps a more contested acceptance that unauthorised interventions may be legitimate if the Security Council is deadlocked. This reformulation of the problem is illuminating in various ways but it does not and cannot resolve the initial ambivalence. As Alex Bellamy demonstrates in relation to Darfur, the language of 'responsibility to protect' can be mobilised to legitimate opposition to intervention in humanitarian emergencies as well as to support it (Bellamy 2005: 40). In Darfur, the responsibility to protect has generally been attached to the Sudanese host government, not with the Security Council, notwithstanding the charges of genocide laid against the host government.

DEBASING THE COINAGE

Equivocation cannot be resolved through the specification of ever more rigorous criteria or through its reformulation in terms of a new legal vocabulary. Its resolution always involves the exercise of political judgement (Ferrara 2007; Fine 2008 forthcoming). This can be illustrated by considering the stance taken by Jürgen Habermas in relation to NATO's intervention in Kosovo and then the US-led invasion of Iraq (Smith 2007a). In general, Habermas endorses the argument that 'confronted with crimes against humanity, the international community must be able to act even with military force, if all other options are exhausted' (quoted in Postel 2002: 1–2). He is in no doubt that the legal doctrine of absolute sovereignty must be revised: 'since human rights would have to be implemented in many cases despite the opposition of national governments, international law's prohibition on intervention is in need of revision' (Habermas 1998: 182). With these principles in mind, he offers a cautious but nonetheless decided defence of NATO's intervention in Kosovo in 1999 and openly condemns the war in Iraq in 2003 (Habermas 2003; Habermas and Derrida 2003a; Smith 2007a).

Habermas attributes his own guarded support for the intervention in Kosovo partly to learning from the history of the UN's inability to protect Bosnian Muslims in the declared 'safe area' of Srebrenica in 1995. His basic case is that notwithstanding the absence of legal authorisation the intervention in Kosovo was right because of the urgency of stopping the ethnic cleansing then taking place. He endorsed the official characterisation of the intervention as an 'armed peace-keeping mission' triggered by an emerging humanitarian catastrophe (Habermas 1999a: 269). While he recognised that the campaign of ethnic cleansing intensified during the bombing, he did not see this as a reason to withdraw support for NATO's actions: 'even though Milosevic is using the NATO air war to force his policy to a bitter conclusion, depressing scenes from the refugee camp do not reverse the relations of causality' (Habermas 1999a: 264). The Kosovo intervention seemed to Habermas to constitute a reasonable attempt to pursue 'the politics of human rights' in the context of a drastically imperfect global order.

Habermas qualified his support by maintaining that the Kosovo intervention should not be treated as a precedent: 'NATO's self-authorization should not be allowed to become the general rule' (Habermas 1999a: 271). It should be seen rather as a stimulus to accelerate the transition from classical international law, based on state sovereignty, to a cosmopolitan legal order. Habermas was concerned over the lack of an explicit UN Security Council resolution to back the use of military force but regarded the situation so grave that military intervention was justified *as an exception*. Whilst he placed great weight on the fact that the intervention was supported by a majority of *democratic* nations, he acknowledged that in a world in which human rights were more firmly embedded within an international legal framework such atrocities would be prosecuted as criminal acts within a legal order. He argued that the realisation of this vision of a cosmopolitan legal order would require sweeping reform of existing arrangements, including the reform of the Security Council and the establishment of the binding jurisprudence of the International Criminal Court and International Court of Justice (Habermas 1999a: 269; 2006: 173–4). As William Smith observes, 'the absence of these institutional arrangements places the politics of human rights in the invidious position of being a mere "anticipation" of the prospective legal order it simultaneously tries to promote' (Smith 2007a).

In 2003 the war in Iraq confirmed Habermas's worst fears that the 'state of exception' was becoming the rule – precisely in the way that the followers of Carl Schmitt might predict (Agamben 2005). The apprehension he expressed during the Kosovo emergency appeared to be actualised in the Bush-Blair doctrine: 'if the regime of international law fails, then the hegemonic imposition of a global liberal order is justified, even by means that are hostile to international law' (Habermas 2003: 365). Habermas maintained that the US, with the support of the UK government, acted as a unilateral hegemon outside of international law and international institutions. There was no convincing authorisation for the war, no immediately pressing humanitarian emergency, no clear indication that the military intervention was a last resort and no efficiency threshold in terms of the harm the military action itself might create. There were deep divisions among democratic nations concerning the legitimacy of the invasion and rather than accelerate the transition from state-based international law to cosmopolitan law the effect of the war was to discredit the very idea of humanitarian military interventions (Roth 2004).

Habermas contrasts the 'Anglo-American' approach to international law, based on an unhealthy mix of strategic instrumentalism, moralism and withdrawal, with the 'European' orientation towards the establishment of a cosmopolitan legal order. A sense of disappointment inhabits the text: 'For half a century the United States could count as the pacemaker for progress on this cosmopolitan path. With the war in Iraq . . . the normative authority of the United States of America lies in ruins' (Habermas 2003a: 365). He views these opposing perspectives on international law as seriously dividing the West and making the development of a cosmopolitan approach within the European Union all the more urgent.

LAW AND JUDGEMENT

There is an admirable boldness to the manner in which Habermas attempts to resolve the ambivalences of the cosmopolitan thinking without losing sight of the cosmopolitan end.[2] He shows an awareness of the need for political judgement rather than rely exclusively on the application of more or less precise legal criteria. For the cosmopolitan to face up to the violence of the age, it is never just a question of mechanically applying pre-given principles to concrete instances; there is always a moment of judgement that mediates between the constitutional principles of international law and their application to particulars. Unlike Rawls, who seems to limit the role of judgement to the application of established principles to particular circumstances, Habermas leaves space for the reflexive elaboration of cosmopolitan principles in the light of our experience of actual interventions. He views experience as a learning process in which we learn to deal with the dangers of slippage, for example, from the making of an exception in international law to the treatment of the exception as the rule or from the judgement of states as outlaw states to the judgement of peoples as outlaw peoples.

Habermas confronts these difficulties but in so doing encounters new difficulties. There is something unsettling about his repeated argument that political judgement is necessary *only* because the constitutionalisation of international law is not yet complete. From this perspective, it might appear that when the transition from classical international law to cosmopolitan law is complete, then the role of political judgement can be surpassed. If this is a vision of finally overcoming political judgement through the procedures of international law, then it is not obviously desirable or plausible. The question is whether political judgement is a stop-gap measure necessary in the absence of clear, concise and authoritative criteria of justification, or rather an irreducible aspect of justifying, authorising and monitoring military interventions. Habermas does not altogether neglect the role of global civil society in publicising the conditions which might make us wish to support or oppose humanitarian military interventions and in influencing those who make the decisions to intervene. The worldwide publicity over the massacre at Srebrenica and the worldwide demonstrations against the invasion of Iraq are cases in point. However, in his vision of the cosmopolitan order to come, deliberations conducted in the public sphere are channelled strictly into avenues of international law, legal judgement, law enforcement and police action.

One can understand the reasoning behind this move to re-position humanitarian military intervention within the confines of international law. It stems from a legitimate attempt to put an end to merely moral justifications of the use of force and to confront the danger of a political power using human rights talk as a spurious justification of military aggression or imperial conquest. The constitutionalisation of international law appears as the cosmopolitan answer to the Schmittian complaint: 'He who invokes humanity wants to cheat.' However, this defensive strategy transfers responsibility for making difficult judgements, in which the values of upholding human rights, seeking peaceful resolution of disputes and respecting national sovereignty are necessarily weighed against one another, from political argument to the legal system. This transfer of responsibility may appear as an attractive strategy in the face, for instance, of unconvincing attempts by the US and UK governments to use justifications of a humanitarian kind for military intervention in Iraq. The perception that this use of humanitarian justifications was in fact an abuse has not only discredited the capacity of the US and its allies to act as bearers of the humanitarian norm but has also cast doubt on the validity of the norm itself. In the face of this dispiriting conclusion the legalisation of the norm appears to have the advantage of rescuing the norm from its political critics by isolating it from the distortions of power.

The difficult question is whether the turn to international law can carry the weight the new cosmopolitanism puts on its shoulders and whether humanitarian military intervention has to be juridified to be justified. I do not wish to argue that Habermas and other cosmopolitans are wrong to defend juridical and procedural mechanisms for justifying, authorising and conducting interventions, only that a *politics* of intervention would not disappear in a regime of 'cosmopolitan law enforcement'. The image that cosmopolitan law can substitute for cosmopolitan political argument forgets that one has to be angry about atrocities being committed somewhere else in the world to want to do something about them and to risk lives to stop them. The unkindest image I sometimes have of legal cosmopolitanism is that we can have the same politicians in power in Western states but that we would go to war for humanitarian reasons because a group of judges say we should.

There is also a residual state-centred quality to this kind of legal imagination. Cosmopolitanism does not have to be attached to the notion that only states, individually or in concert, have the responsibility to protect people against organised terror, expulsion and annihilation. The responsibility to protect has a more universal application within cosmopolitan thought. It might include, for instance, publicity and support for civil rights movements, free trade unions, women's equality movements and democratic political parties in atrocity-committing regimes, and safe havens for refugees in search of asylum from these regimes, rather than or in addition to state-based armed interventions. We should not forget that genocide in Rwanda was terminated neither by Western states nor by the UN but in this case by the Rwandese Patriotic Front and Army.

Finally, humanitarian military interventions are likely to give rise to reactive forms of resistance in the name of anti-imperialism. It is a matter of political judgement, however, whether such 'resistance' is justified. Today we see a resistance which increasingly glorifies violence, demonises its enemies and loses touch with the values of political democracy and post-traditional civil society. In these circumstances, cosmopolitanism involves not only an appeal to the constitutional principles of international law but a political critique of the world view which feeds the sheer negativity of this form of resistence.

6

COSMOPOLITANISM
AND PUNISHMENT
Prosecuting crimes against humanity

The prosecution of crimes against humanity is often given pride of place within the new cosmopolitanism as the marker not only of the transition from classical international law to cosmopolitan law but of the emergence more broadly of a cosmopolitan consciousness that stretches across national boundaries. What makes this aspect of international criminal justice so significant for cosmopolitanism is that the idea of crimes against humanity refers to 'crimes that can be committed completely within one state's borders by members of that state against other members of that same state' and therefore 'challenges the traditional understanding of a state's exclusive pre-rogative over crimes committed within its borders' (May 2006: 349). And yet the normative standing of this legal institution has been challenged from all sides: by those who denigrate the prosecution of crimes against humanity as merely 'victors' justice' in a legal cloth; by those who see the criminalisation of individuals as an irrelevance in relation to larger issues of responsibility and justice; and those who are suspicious of codified abstractions dissolving the particular experience of horror shared by the victims. In the face of these criticisms the characteristic response of the new cosmopolitanism is to look to the completion of the transition to cosmopolitan law: to develop an international criminal court, to specify the content of crimes against humanity, consolidate the status of this crime within international criminal law, establish an international police force to apprehend suspects, and construct a system of impartial adjudication and punishment. I suggest, however, that this predominantly legal response to the normative fragility of the law of crimes against humanity should also address the inter-connections of law and politics. Instead of exploring the relation between cosmopolitan law and politics, the juridical approach seeks to isolate the law from politics and elevate it above politics. I shall argue that cosmopolitan social theory entails a way of understanding crimes against humanity which from the start traces the ties that bind law to politics and politics to law.

The exemplar of this approach to cosmopolitanism whose work I shall discuss in this chapter is the political theorist, Hannah Arendt. Her investigations into the *actuality* of crimes against humanity and the construction of an anti-totalitarian politics capable of facing up to their 'horrible originality' provide my starting point. More specifically, her accounts of the Nuremberg trials after the Second World War and 15 years later the trial of Adolf Eichmann, the official in charge of transporting Jews to the death camps, provide a rich seam of analysis from which I shall seek to extract what I would call a 'worldly cosmopolitanism' (Arendt 1977b, 1994, 2003; Arendt and Jaspers 1992; Arendt and McCarthy 1995). Arendt took into account competing renditions of crimes against humanity: the idealisation of cosmopolitan law in the work of Karl Jaspers; the dismissal of cosmopolitan law as victors' justice in the work of Carl Schmitt; the downplaying of cosmopolitan law in relation to larger issues of responsibility in the work of Martin Heidegger; the subordination of cosmopolitan law to the uniqueness of the Holocaust in the work of Gershom Scholem. Worldly cosmopolitanism does not necessarily entail empathy with these alternative standpoints, but it seeks to capture the element of 'truth' in what others have to say and draw it into our own thinking. My contention is that Arendt's threefold engagement with crimes against humanity – with the actuality of the crimes themselves, with the prosecution of the crimes after the event and with the differing standpoints from which others 'see' both the crimes themselves and their prosecution – remains as instructive for our understanding of cosmopolitan social theory as it is for current debates on international criminal justice.

ARENDT AND JASPERS: NUREMBERG

The formative moment in contemporary cosmopolitanism was the institution of the law of 'crimes against humanity' in the Nuremberg Charter and then its application in the Nuremberg Tribunal. The category of crimes against humanity was conceived as a supplement to existing crimes in international criminal law, 'war crimes' and 'crimes against peace', made necessary by the unprecedented levels of organised violence directed against civilians. The concept was not entirely new. Its pre-history goes back to the charge of 'crimes against humanity and civilization' laid at the Turkish government for the massacre of Armenians in 1915. It was reformulated by international lawyers in the latter part of the Second World War to make it possible for a court of law to consider such crimes as those that were being committed in the so-called 'final solution of the Jewish question' (Marrus 1997: 185–7).

Why has this innovation in international criminal justice caught the cosmopolitan imagination? An answer to this question is to be found in *The Question of German Guilt* written in 1945 by the philosopher and friend of Arendt, Karl Jaspers. Jaspers discerned among the ruins of Nuremberg 'a barely perceptible dawn' – the actualisation of the vision of cosmopolitan order first conceived by Kant (Jaspers 1961). His argument may be reconstructed around the following eight points. First, the prosecution of crimes against humanity transcended established principles of national sovereignty, which had too long put a 'halo' around heads of states and made them inviolable to prosecution. Second, it announced that individuals acting within the legality of their own state could nonetheless be tried as criminals and that service to the state no longer exonerates any official in any bureaucracy or any scientist in any laboratory from personal responsibility. Third, it removed the excuse of 'only obeying orders' from perpetrators and it held those who sit behind desks planning atrocities as guilty as those who participate directly in their execution. Fourth, it enabled a distinction to be made between the criminally guilty and the indefinite number of others who were capable of co-operating under orders but not guilty in a criminal sense. Fifth, it provided a lawful alternative to the barbarities of collective punishment. Sixth, it extended the notion of criminal guilt in international law beyond that of war guilt and made visible the unprecedented levels of violence against civilians that had come into existence. Seventh, by treating mass murderers as mere criminals it represented them in their 'total banality' and deprived them of that 'streak of satanic greatness' with which they might otherwise have been endowed. Finally, it signified that crimes committed against one set of people, be it Jews, Poles or Roma, are an affront not only to these particular people but to humanity as a whole and that humanity has a duty to hold to account those who commit them. This list is not exhaustive but it indicates why Jaspers was moved to describe the Nuremberg Charter as 'a feeble, ambiguous harbinger of a world order the need of which mankind is beginning to feel' (Jaspers 1961: 60).

In correspondence with Jaspers, Arendt offered a more equivocal assessment. She endorsed the prosecution of crimes against humanity as a crucial step in the direction of universal responsibility. However, her enthusiasm for the *law* of crimes against humanity was weighed against the overwhelming eventfulness of the crimes themselves. She suggested that the enormity of Nazi crimes explode the limits of the law:

> For these crimes, no punishment is severe enough . . . That is, their guilt, in contrast to all criminal guilt, oversteps and shatters any and all legal systems . . . We are simply not equipped to deal, on a human, political level, with a guilt that is beyond crime . . . The Germans are burdened now with thousands or tens of thousands or hundreds of thousands of people who cannot be adequately punished within the legal system.
>
> (Arendt and Jaspers 1992: 54)

She maintained that criminal law is not equipped to deal with the difference between 'a man who sets out to murder his old aunt' and 'people who without considering the economic usefulness of their actions at all ... built factories to produce corpses'. There was something about *this* guilt that oversteps all legal systems. She underlined the disproportion between the small number of Nazis who could be treated as criminally guilty and the vast numbers of individuals implicated in conceiving, planning and executing the Final Solution. When a machinery of mass murder impels practically everyone to participate in crime, the distinction between the guilty and the innocent is effaced: 'Where all are guilty, nobody in the last analysis can be judged' (Arendt and Jaspers 1992: 125). She doubted that this exercise in criminal law would instil in Germans a sense of responsibility for what had been done to Jews. German people, she wrote, did not in general regard themselves as murderers and the punishment of war criminals, rather than construct a new sense of responsibility, provoked in them feelings of resentment and betrayal. Its effect was to exonerate all Germans but the accused of their guilt.

I would present the difference between Arendt and Jaspers in this way. Jaspers acknowledged that the Nuremberg trials were not yet based on a global legal order and that the category of crimes against humanity was still contained within a national framework. The deficiencies of Nuremberg were that the charge of crimes against humanity was sparingly used by prosecutors; crimes against humanity were tied to the conduct of war; the tribunal could only consider crimes committed by Germans and excluded in principle those committed by the allied powers; and the tribunal itself was a multinational body established by the victorious powers and not an international tribunal. For Jaspers, the shortcoming of the tribunal lay in its reluctance to shake the foundations of national sovereignty (Deak 1993; Douglas 2001; Salter 1999). However, he saw it as the first sign of a more general re-evaluation of responsibility after Nazism, whose aim was not just to re-orient the pariah nation, Germany, back to the main current of Western humanism but to renew the tradition of Western humanism itself. Even if the norms established in international criminal law were not yet universalised, they were universalisable.

Arendt shared Jaspers' cosmopolitan vision of universal responsibility. In language reminiscent of Søren Kierkegaard, she looked to a time when

> human beings would assume responsibility for all crimes committed by human beings, in which no one people are assigned a monopoly of guilt and none considers itself superior, in which good citizens would not shrink back in horror at German crimes and declare 'Thank God, I am not like that', but rather recognise in fear and trembling the incalculable evil which humanity is capable of and fight fearlessly, uncompromisingly, everywhere against it.
>
> (Arendt 1994: 132)

Arendt's appeal to universal responsibility served less to indicate the *legal* limitations of international criminal justice, limitations that

could be surpassed, than a conflict between the universal significance of the prosecution of crimes against humanity and the moral
division of the world into the poles of German barbarism and allied
innocence. The prosecution of crimes against humanity is Janus-
faced: on the one hand, it overcomes the impunity of rulers; on
the other, it threatens to stigmatise the enemy in ways that would
serve only to reinforce the old national framework. While Jaspers
addressed the defects of Nuremberg in juridical terms of law's progression, Arendt's concern was that the law was neither working to
create a sense of responsibility among Germans nor to break the
image of the 'unspeakable Nazi beast'.

The differences between Jaspers and Arendt should not be overstated, since both saw the majesty of international law in some sense
realised at Nuremberg. The more salient point, perhaps, is that the
cosmopolitan precedent established at Nuremberg quickly evaporated with the onset of the cold war – not because crimes against
humanity disappeared from the world but because the political
sensibility that nurtured their prosecution was no longer present.
For 40 years or more the idea of 'crimes against humanity' returned
to the backburner of world history, sustained only among a few
radical intellectuals of an anti-totalitarian persuasion and some civil
society groupings committed to holding to account perpetrators of
atrocities, no matter how high their status.[1] The major powers either
withdrew from international criminal law or, as in the Auschwitz
trials of 1963, turned to domestic legislation.[2] There was something
premature in any cosmopolitan faith in law's progress. The ideals
represented at Nuremberg were more like a flash of light prior to
the Cold War than a transition to a new cosmopolitan order.

ARENDT AND JASPERS: THE EICHMANN TRIAL

When we move forward fifteen years from Nuremberg to Jerusalem,
we find a shift of emphasis in both Jaspers and Arendt. Jaspers
expressed equivocation about a trial he saw falling far short of
the ideals of legal cosmopolitanism. He criticised the kidnapping
of Eichmann from Argentina as having no legal justification. He
criticised the use of a national court on the grounds that 'it is a
task for humanity, not for an individual national state' to pass judgement on crimes against humanity. He criticised the use of an *Israeli*

court, arguing that punishment might appear more like vengeance than law. He maintained that 'something other than law is at issue here' and to address it in exclusively legal terms was a mistake (Arendt and Jaspers 1992: 410–19; Jaspers 2006). Arendt was less impressed by legalistic objections. She was unwilling to condemn the kidnapping of a man indicted at Nuremberg for crimes against humanity – particularly from a country with such a bad record of extradition as Argentina. She was unwilling to condemn the use of an Israeli court: many of the surviving Jewish victims lived there, Eichmann was charged with the mass murder of Jews, and in any event there was no international court. She repudiated the argument echoed by Eichmann's counsel that as a Jewish institution the court had a political interest in the outcome and could not therefore be relied upon to deliver justice. She acknowledged that bigger issues were at stake than are containable within a purely legal framework – the nature of evil, totalitarianism, political anti-Semitism – but this was no reason to deny the validity of prosecuting Eichmann. In any event there were no other tools to hand except legal ones with which to judge Eichmann (Arendt and Jaspers 1992: 417).

Arendt's reservations over the Eichmann trial were of another kind. They had to do with losing sight of the universalistic promise of prosecuting crimes against humanity. She heard the voice of Jewish nationalism in the prosecution's contention that only in Israel could a Jew be safe, in its camouflaging of ethnic distinctions in Israeli society, in its refusal to face up to the complicity of Jewish community leaders in the administration of the Final Solution, and not least in the fact that Eichmann was charged not only with crimes against humanity but more centrally with 'crimes against the Jewish people'. In permitting this newly constructed offence Arendt argued that the court failed to understand that

> the physical extermination of the Jewish people was a crime against humanity perpetrated on the body of the Jewish people, and that only the choice of victims, not the nature of the crime, could be derived from the long history of Jew-hatred and antisemitism.
>
> (Arendt 1977b: 269)

This was the nub of the issue for Arendt: the attempted extermination of the Jewish people was not to be understood as the culmination of a long line of persecutory acts against Jews, rather it was 'an attack upon human diversity as such, that is, upon a characteristic of the "human status" without which the very words "mankind" or "humanity" would be devoid of meaning' (Arendt 1977b: 268–9). The court failed to understand that in destroying an ethnic group humankind in its entirety might be 'grievously hurt and endangered' (Arendt 1977b: 276). Arendt's concern was that the court and especially the prosecutor, Gideon Hausner, were reinforcing the very situation that the idea of crimes against humanity had sought to correct – the breaking up of the human race into a multitude of competing nations.

Arendt argued that the political shortcomings of the trial dovetailed with its legal shortcomings. The main business of any criminal trial, she argued, is to 'weigh up the charges, render judgement and mete out due punishment'. However, in this trial the prosecutor could not resist the temptation to subordinate legal justice to moral ends. He appealed to Jewish rather than secular legality, he resorted to biblical conceptions of vengeance, he subsumed legal criteria of relevance to the unchecked testimony of survivor-witnesses, and he portrayed them all as Jewish heroes. Arendt acknowledged the extra-legal achievements of the trial, not least its exposure to public scrutiny of the destruction of European Jewry and the space it provided for survivor-witnesses to have their say in public, but she maintained that these ends would not be served if justice were not done and be seen to be done. It is important not to overstate Arendt's criticisms. The failures of the Eichmann trial, as she put it, were 'neither in kind nor in degree greater than the failures of the Nuremberg trials or the successor trials in other European countries' (Arendt 1977b: 274). Justice was done even if the principal crime could not be found in the law books. The difference between Arendt and Jaspers should not be overstated. Both attempt to construct a cosmopolitan point of view on the trial and both supported the construction of an international criminal court. However, while Jaspers measured the trial against a legal ideal and found it wanting, Arendt drew hard-headed judgements from deeply equivocal material.

STRATEGIES OF DENIAL

The cosmopolitan analysis put forward by both Jaspers and Arendt contrast markedly with strategies of denial adopted by the defendants themselves as well as by onlookers and historians sceptical of the significance of this innovation in international criminal justice. The jurist Carl Schmitt, himself interrogated at Nuremberg, quipped that a 'crime against humanity' is one committed by Germans while a 'crime for humanity' is committed by Americans. He treated the prosecution of crimes against humanity as a prime example of 'victors' justice' in a juridical disguise which served only to construct the defeated enemy as 'inhuman' (Salter 1999).[3]

One strategy was to deny the validity of the law on the grounds that it was enacted by four victorious military powers and not by an authorised international legislature, it used vague phrases like 'other inhumane acts' as part of its lexicon, it was retrospectively applied to acts committed prior to the law itself, and it excluded equivalent crimes committed by the victorious powers (Deak 1993). Since the law violated formal principles of legality – that it be authoritative in its origins, general in its application, specific in its formulation and non-retroactive in its enforcement – it was argued that it was not properly speaking law at all (Kirchheimer 1969; Neumann 1942). Another strategy was to claim that acts labelled 'crimes against humanity' are normal routines of power in the international arena, not fundamentally different from other acts of power not so labelled. In the later case of Klaus Barbie, 'the butcher of Lyons', his lawyers based their defence on the argument that their client's actions as police chief during the occupation were merely a case of 'white Europeans' doing to other 'white Europeans' what all white Europeans have routinely done to black non-Europeans and that by putting Barbie on trial the French were camouflaging their colonial history (Finkielkraut 1992). A third strategy was to deny personal responsibility on the grounds that perpetrators of crimes against humanity have no choice but to obey orders and cannot, therefore, be held guilty of the crimes committed. Appeal was made to external constraints to which the perpetrators were subjected: if the choice facing an individual is that of 'kill or be killed', it is only in a formal sense that an individual is responsible for his or her actions. Appeal was also made to the *internal* constraints faced by the accused.

Eichmann argued that since the command of the Führer was the 'absolute centre' of the legal system, he simply could not have acted otherwise despite bearing no ill feelings towards his victims.

Martin Heidegger employed similar strategies of denial when called upon by Herbert Marcuse to disavow the Nazi regime. What the Nazis did to the Jews was no worse, he wrote, than what the Russians did to the Germans. He maintained that the 'manufacture of corpses in gas chambers and extermination camps' deserves no more attention than other practices of modern technology, like 'a motorised food-industry', which are 'in essence – the same'. He compared 'those who were liquidated inconspicuously in extermi- nation camps' to 'the millions of impoverished people right now . . . perishing from hunger in China' and distinguished only between those 'capable of enduring death in its essence' and those who merely 'succumb' and are 'done in' (Lang 1997; Rabinbach 1997). A more interesting perspective, however, is apparent in his 'Letter on Humanism' (1947). Written as a response to Sartre's credo of absolute individual responsibility, which allows no excuses for one's actions, not even Abraham acting under the command of God, Heidegger relocated humanism as a metaphysics of the subject that denies the historicality and finite freedom of human existence (Heidegger 1976: 219). Humanism elevates the human being as master of all things. It constructs a technological relation to the world based on the domination of nature and people. Heidegger insisted that when he spoke against humanism, his argument was not designed to be destructive. It 'in no way implies a defence of the inhuman, but rather opens other vistas' (Heidegger 1976: 250). It does not declare humanism false but inadequate to the task of realis- ing 'the proper dignity of man'. It does not align itself 'against the humane' or advocate 'the inhuman' but maintains only that human- ism 'does not set the *humanitas* of man high enough' (Heidegger 1976: 233). Nazism became a catastrophe because it turned oppo- sition to humanism into an advocacy of the inhuman. Heidegger said he did not wish to do away with laws that 'hold human beings together ever so tenuously' but rather 'to think the humanity of *homo humanus* . . . without humanism' (Heidegger 1976: 254). If Schmitt stood for the atrophy of responsibility, Heidegger stood for its hypertrophy. In either case ordinary legal responsibility appeared hard to sustain.

In response to these strategies of denial Jaspers heard only the voice of hypocrisy and evasion. For Arendt, their more troubling aspect lay in the 'truth' they contained. The prosecution of crimes against humanity can serve to demonise the enemy, it can conceal the crimes of the victors, it can reinforce national conceptions of guilt and innocence, it can absolve the ordinary citizen of responsibility, it can label people arbitrarily and it can draw attention away from the larger ethical issues at stake. Even the epithet 'victors' justice' expresses the truth that there is no court in the world that is not the result of a prior victory. Resentment may be fuelled by a justified sense of the gulf between the humanitarian standards powerful nations purport to respect and the violence they reveal in practice.

Arendt noted the 'conspicuous helplessness the judges experienced when they were confronted with the task they could least escape ... understanding the criminal whom they had come to judge'. Eichmann was neither perverted nor sadistic but terrifyingly normal: 'this new type of criminal ... commits his crimes under circumstances that make it well-nigh impossible for him to know or to feel that he is doing wrong' (Arendt 1977b: 276). Other than personal ambition he seemed to have no motives. It was as if 'sheer thoughtlessness ... predisposed him to become one of the greatest criminals of that period' (Arendt 1977b: 288). Eichmann's defence was that he was a cog in a machine, to which Arendt observed that 'the whole cog theory is *legally* pointless' because in a trial 'all the cogs in the machinery, no matter how insignificant, are in court forthwith transformed back into perpetrators, that is to say, into human beings' (Arendt 1977b: 289). The alternative was not attractive: to 'judge and even ... condemn ... trends, or whole groups of people – the larger the better' in such a way that 'distinctions can no longer be made, names no longer named' (Arendt 1977b: 296). As Arendt put it, we have to overcome 'the reluctance evident everywhere to make judgments in terms of individual moral responsibility' (Arendt 1977b: 297).

Arendt was, mistakenly in my view, critical of sociology for accepting too readily that the essence of modern bureaucracy is 'to make functionaries and mere cogs ... out of men, and thus to dehumanise them' (Arendt 1977b: 289).[4] In fact, in Weber's conception of bureaucracy officials *are* responsible for their actions, and part of the immense power of bureaucracy is based on a responsibility for decision-making and rule interpretation that is distributed throughout the hierarchy. If crimes against humanity were organised by a typical modern bureaucracy, individuals would have been expected to take responsibility for the tasks assigned to them and the leadership could not have relied on employees to perpetrate murder simply as cogs in a machine. The process of following a rule is mediated through consciousness and the *ethos* of public service is the oil that allows the machine to run smoothly. Rules are nothing without interpretation and application. Arendt argued, however, that the form of organisation involved in crimes against humanity was radically different from the Weberian model of legal-rational bureaucracy. Movement rather than structure was its essence. There was an intermeshing of state and party institutions. Duplication was apparent in the many police apparatuses all doing similar work, spying on the population and on each other, without any clear knowledge of who will be rewarded and who purged. In the complexities of totalitarian domination all were 'equal with respect to each other and no one belonging to one group owed obedience to a superior officer of another' (Arendt 1977b: 71). The categorical imperative of the *Führerprinkip* was: 'Act in such a way as the Führer, if he knew your action, would approve it' (Arendt 1977b: 136). This was not a principle of bureaucracy organised on the basis of formal rules within a structured hierarchy; the allegiance of the official was not owed to his or her immediate superior but to the leader. To be sure, *elements* of bureaucracy were retained: people were numbered and processed by bureaucratic-type machines; there were papers, form filling, official stamps, mug shots and files kept on individuals. But behind the simulacrum of bureaucracy we find no hierarchy of command or system of rules recognisable to a student of Weber. Officials in positions of authority could be denounced and replaced by juniors; one apparatus was liable to be liquidated in favour of another; the stability and hierarchy of genuine bureaucracy were absent.

Arendt herself was equivocal about the effects of totalitarian organisation on personal responsibility (Lefort 1986). It is certainly arguable, however, that the individual responsibility of the official was greater under the 'leader principle' than in a regulated hierarchical bureaucracy in which responsibility and authority are distributed according to plan. To grasp the will of the Führer demanded zeal and creativity far in excess of the plodding bureaucrat and wide latitude given to sub-leaders for the execution of policies. Each holder of position was responsible for the activities of subordinates, even in cases of disobedience and failure. Individuals were not generally *forced* into the formations that perpetrated crimes against humanity and members of murderous police battalions (*Einsatzgruppen*), for example, were given the opportunity to withdraw from the killing actions (Browning 1993). Under the 'leader principle' authority worked through the will of every member to know and act in accordance with the will of the leader and take responsibility for all the decisions taken in their field of operation.

In short, responsibility for crimes against humanity is more than a legal fiction; it is a form of social organisation and the image of bureaucracy devoid of human subjectivity is a chimera. Actors may present themselves *as if* they were cogs in a machine but the responsibility of the doer for his deed does not thereby vanish. Eichmann was the archetype of this new type of bourgeois, not the Kantian individual who prides himself on thinking for himself but the 'mass man' who sees himself as an employee without agency. Eichmann said in court he had read Kant's *Critique of Practical Reason* and came up with a roughly correct version of the categorical imperative: 'I meant by my remark about Kant that the principle of my will must always be such that it can become the principle of general laws' (Arendt 1977b: 136). However, once charged with carrying out the Final Solution, Eichmann claimed that he *ceased* to live according to Kantian principles and became a mere employee working under orders. Since he was 'only doing his job' and acting 'in a professional capacity', he could not be regarded as a murderer. We have to distinguish between Eichmann's self-presentation as a cog in a machine and his actual responsibility for the crimes he committed.

Arendt also takes seriously the idea of a crime being *against humanity*. She described the Nazi death camps as an organised attempt to 'eradicate the concept of the human being'. What was at stake was not only 'the blotting out of whole peoples, the "clearance" of whole regions of their native population', but also the destruction of 'the human status' (Arendt 1977b: 257). The idea of being 'against humanity' percolates through Arendt's account of modern politics:

> Something seems to be involved in modern politics that actually should never be involved in politics as we used to understand it, namely all or nothing – all, and that is an undetermined infinity of forms, of human living together, or nothing, for a victory of the concentration camp system would mean the same inexorable doom for human beings as the use of the hydrogen bomb would for the human race.
>
> (Arendt 1979)

Or again:

> These modern, state-employed mass murderers must be prosecuted because they violated the order of mankind, and not because they killed millions of people. Nothing is more pernicious to an understanding of these new crimes, or stands in the way of the emergence of an international penal code that could take care of them, than the common illusion that the crime of murder and the crime of genocide are essentially the same, and that the latter therefore is 'no new crime properly speaking'.
>
> (Arendt 1977b: 272)

Death camps were an attempt not only to murder *en masse* human beings of a certain stripe but also to 'eradicate the idea of humanity'. They functioned to eliminate 'spontaneity itself as an expression of human behaviour', to transform 'the human personality into a mere thing', to destroy 'all sign of human plurality', to realise the supposition that 'all men have become equally superfluous' (Arendt 1979: 439–59). They constituted 'an attack upon human diversity as such, that is, upon a characteristic of the "human status" without which the very words "mankind" or "humanity" would be devoid of meaning' (Arendt 1977b: 268–9).

Arendt acknowledged that in speaking of crimes against humanity international lawyers have to deal with human propensities that are 'very difficult to grasp juridically' and there has indeed been much debate about what is meant by the term 'against humanity' (May 2005). Arendt too found it difficult to grasp. In using the term 'humanity' she declared she did not have in mind a fixed conception of human nature: 'Nothing entitles us to assume that man has a nature or essence in the same sense as other things' (Arendt 1958: 9). She preferred the language of 'human status' to 'human nature' because it refers to 'the sum total of human activities and capabilities which correspond to the human condition' (Arendt 1958: 10). I think we need to make a further step. Once we think of 'humanity' in terms of a certain status in the world, we can also address its historicity. The idea of the human status originated in the ancient world as a particular status that contrasted with that of slaves, foreigners and women. In the modern world it is generalised as the status of all human beings. The anthropologist, Claude Lévi-Strauss, observed:

> The concept of an all inclusive humanity, which makes no distinction between races or cultures, appeared very late in the history of mankind and did not spread very widely across the globe. What is more, as proved by recent events, even in one region where it seems most developed, it has not escaped periods of regression and ambiguity. For the majority of the human species, and for tens of thousands of years, the idea that humanity includes every human being on the face of the earth does not exist at all.
>
> (Lévi-Strauss 1983: 329; cited in Finkielkraut 2001: 5)

Crimes against humanity are crimes committed to undo this accomplishment of the modern age and conceptually they may be distinguished from the much longer history of crimes committed in the name of humanity: for example, against colonial subjects excluded from the status of human being by virtue of their 'idolatry', 'coarseness of intelligence' or the 'evil they inflict on one another' (Mehta 1999). In practice the dividing line is difficult to define.

What I take from Arendt is this: it is justified to prosecute crimes against humanity because some crimes are against humanity and individuals are responsible for them. Arendt referred to Eichmann through a category of Roman law, *hostis generis humani*, enemy of the human status. Her point was not to portray Eichmann as an inhuman beast outside of human community. On the contrary, the prosecution revealed Eichmann to be human, all too human. The prosecution of crimes against humanity is designed not to demonise the accused (Norrie 2006) but to humanise them, to treat them as responsible human beings. The history of the idea of 'crimes against humanity' in international criminal justice is a story of opportunities and lost opportunities whose outcome is as dependent on the judgement of ordinary citizens, like Arendt, as on the formalities of law and legal process. The cosmopolitan point of view is not simply to validate international criminal justice but to reconcile a commitment to this transformative political project with recognition of the world as it actually exists (Smith 2007a).

Arendt's 'worldly cosmopolitanism', as I have put it, addresses the intersection of law and politics in a style that recognises that there is more to international criminal justice than 'the unfolding of law's master plan'. It acknowledges that the universalistic import of prosecuting crimes against humanity can revert to a logic of demonisation, that justice can be subordinated to extra-legal ends, that a prosecution can end up looking more like a show trial than a court of law, that hostility to the idea of 'humanity' is more than a pathological outburst of nihilism (Koskenniemi 2002). Worldly cosmopolitanism is not forged simply through the progression of legal and institutional forms but through our capacity as actors in the public sphere to come to terms with our cosmopolitan existence. This means that when we judge and act in political matters, we take our bearings 'from the idea, not the actuality, of being a world citizen' (Arendt 1992: 76). In her reflections on crimes against humanity Arendt offers an illustration, however fractured, of what it is to think as a cosmopolitan citizen in a world in which cosmopolitanism is no more than a flash of light in dark times.

COSMOPOLITANISM AND HOLOCAUST UNIQUENESS

The elaboration of the cosmopolitan point of view may be pursued by contrasting it with another reading of crimes against the Jewish people that also surfaced in the Eichmann trial. The philosopher, Gershom Scholem, picked up on Arendt's discussion of evil and her use of a now familiar term, 'banality of evil':

> Your thesis concerning the 'banality of evil' . . . underlies your entire argument. This new thesis strikes me as a catchword; it does not impress me, certainly, as the product of profound analysis – an analysis such as you give us so convincingly . . . in

your book on totalitarianism. At that time you had not yet made your discovery . . . that evil is banal. Of that 'radical evil' to which your then analysis bore such eloquent and erudite witness, nothing remains but this slogan . . .

(Arendt 1978a: 245)

Scholem accused Arendt of trivializing the destruction of European Jewry when she abandoned the language of 'radical evil' she had used in *The Origins of Totalitarianism* to describe the death camps. Arendt acknowledged that Scholem was right in one respect:

You are quite right: I changed my mind and do no longer speak of 'radical evil' . . . It is indeed my opinion now that evil is never 'radical', that it is only extreme, and that it possesses neither depth nor any demonic dimension. It can overgrow and lay waste the whole world precisely because it spreads like a fungus on the surface. It is 'thought-defying' . . . because thought tries to reach some depth, to go to the roots, and the moment it concerns itself with evil, it is frustrated because there is nothing. That is its 'banality'. Only the good has depth and can be radical.

(Arendt 1978a: 250–1)

Arendt wrote of 'the appearance of radical evil' because the death camps lacked any 'humanly understandable sinful motives', such as 'self-interest, greed, covetousness, resentment, lust for power, and cowardice' (Arendt 1958: 241). The Eichmann case revealed, however, that the perpetrators of horror can be thoroughly pedestrian individuals motivated by little more than careerism. Although his deeds were monstrous, the doer was 'ordinary, commonplace, and neither demonic nor monstrous' (Arendt 1977b: 3–4). She was not trying to trivialise the Holocaust, she was trying to understand the gulf between agency and action that makes such events possible (Bernstein 1996: 138).

Banality of evil involves a cluster of connotations with family resemblance to one another. It indicates that it requires no depth to destroy and that the Final Solution substituted destruction of 'the Jews' for any vision Nazism might once have had of reconstructing Europe. It is a rejoinder to conventional images of the 'Nazi monster', signifying a refusal to dehumanise the perpetrator in return for the perpetrator's dehumanisation of his victims. It refuses to see the perpetrator as having nothing in common with ourselves.[5] It reveals that evil is not outside the range of human understanding, judgement and punishment. Scholem's hostility was the expression of another sensibility: one which fashioned the concepts of the 'Holocaust' and 'Shoah' out of the raw materials of Jewish theology to name this singular and incomparable event and remove it from the terrain of human understanding and judgement.[6] Arendt speculated on the possibility of a catastrophe so consuming as to destroy our capacity for understanding: 'how can we measure length if we do not have a yardstick, how could we count things without the notion of numbers?' The Holocaust might have been like this if the voice of resistance were silenced and if the attempt to exterminate Jews had been carried to a successful conclusion. But this thought-experiment is counterfactual: it highlights the limitations of 'an experiment which requires global control in order to show conclusive results' (Arendt 1979: 459). We can perhaps envisage a catastrophe so terrible as to exterminate the possibility of 'knowing' the catastrophe itself or judging those responsible for it, but the Holocaust left behind survivors, witnesses, documents, traces and perpetrators.[7] Our *capacity* both to understand and to judge survived.

The seemingly arcane distinction between 'radical evil' and 'banality of evil' became charged because these terms stood proxy for a conflict between two ways of thinking: one which we might term 'Holocaust uniqueness' and the other 'worldly cosmopolitanism'. Crimes against humanity can appear beyond human comprehension. It seems senseless to punish innocent people, to fail to keep them in a condition in which profitable work might be extorted from them, to be intent on terrifying a completely subdued population. Arendt wrote: 'It was as though the Nazis were convinced that it was of greater importance to run extermination factories than to win the war' (Arendt 1992: 233). The gas chambers did not benefit anybody. They did not seem to have any definite purpose. The office of Himmler issued one order after another 'warning the military commanders . . . that no economic or military considerations were to interfere with the extermination programme' (Arendt 1992: 236). The spirit of Arendt's response to Scholem is this. Because we can find no *rational* explanation for such phenomena, we are tempted to declare them beyond human understanding. However, the cosmopolitan institution is to resist this temptation and through judgement and understanding to reconstruct the idea of humanity in the face its eradication.

7

COSMOPOLITANISM AND THE LIFE OF THE MIND

The critique of nihilism[1]

This chapter, as the title suggests, draws self-consciously on a reconstruction of Hannah Arendt's *The Life of the Mind*. I refer to this text in part to affirm the importance of the life of the mind in any vision of cosmopolitan order and in part to explore the critical role cosmopolitanism plays in understanding the life of the mind as it is currently lived. My thesis is that Arendt's perplexing, late and unfinished text offers not only a defence of the life of the mind but also a diagnosis of the pathologies of the life of the modern mind. It is, if you wish, a critique of modern reason.

The book itself was unfinished. Judgement, or judging, was to be its last section but was never written. We have the first two sections of *The Life of the Mind*, those on *Thinking* and *Willing*, and fragments of discussion on the nature of judgement drawn from Arendt's *Lectures on Kant's Critique of Judgment* and various other political and cultural essays.[2] Curiously, this has not stopped many commentators from representing this 'incomplete' work on judging as the apex of Arendt's contribution to political thought (Beiner in Arendt 1992). 'The faculty of judgment played a pre-eminent role in Hannah Arendt's political and moral thought', writes Albrecht

Wellmer (2001: 165).[3] This may be true but it is a little strange to pick out this one radically incomplete aspect of Arendt's political thought when she proffered such highly developed analyses of other subjects such as totalitarianism, anti-Semitism, imperialism, crimes against humanity, revolution and the public sphere. Something special is being accorded to the faculty of judgement, or rather to one type of judgement, reflective judgement, and there is a sense that either Arendt herself or her later commentators have seen in reflective judgement a kind of philosopher's stone that will open the secrets of political thought.

Any reconstruction of *The Life of the Mind* has to address what Arendt was doing in the book as a whole. To 'complete' in any satisfactory sense the unfinished section of this book, we need to extract the *method* present within Arendt's analysis of the life of the mind as a whole, see how she applies this method to the study of thinking and willing, and then extend this method to the subject of judging. This is no easy matter – particularly as the sections on *Thinking* and *Willing* have a very different character.[4] Yet if we are to reconstruct the unwritten final section of *The Life of the Mind* on judging, we need to have an idea of what the work as a whole is doing and how the different parts relate internally to one another.

Putting aside for a brief moment any doubts we might have about the treatment of thinking, willing and judging as distinct *faculties*, let me put forward the following proposition about the relationship between thinking, willing and judging as Arendt conceived, or more accurately *might have* conceived it. My proposition is that Arendt was a cosmopolitan thinker in this respect, that she had some notion of a possible harmony between these 'faculties' of the mind; but she saw any such harmony severely jeopardised in the modern world where the activities of thinking, willing and judging are radically differentiated, specialised and in constant risk of isolation. The danger she saw lies both in the atrophy and in the hypertrophy of one or more of these faculties. If modernity in some sense constitutes the differentiation of the faculties and allows for the specialisation of thought, will and judgement as discrete elements in a larger division of mental labour, modernity also creates the pathogenic conditions for the underdevelopment of some of these faculties of the mind and the overdevelopment of others. It is an instance, if you like, of combined and uneven development of the faculties of the mind.

The focus of Arendt's study is on the pathologies of the life of the *modern* mind. When we read the text of *The Life of the Mind*, it becomes clear that Arendt sees the 'faculties' of thinking and willing as containing deep inner contradictions and there is no reason to suppose that her treatment of judging would be any different. While the isolation of thinking, willing and judging in the modern division of intellectual labour brings to the fore the contradictions latent within each of these faculties, Arendt's underlying motif is that it is only through the unity of the life of the mind that the contradictions internal to one faculty can be mediated by another. In other words, we might say that the angle from which Arendt approaches her critique of the life of the mind as a whole is that of understanding the distorted form of modernisation that results from the division of the life of the mind into distinct and opposing faculties.[5]

This reading of the text resists any temptation to rationalise the division of the mind into 'faculties' or reconstruct Arendt's missing section on judgement on this basis. It resists in particular the temptation to locate the text within a teleological framework which I find incompatible with Arendt's aporetic way of thinking. We cannot, for instance, elevate *thinking* as the good faculty of the mind, demote *willing* as the bad and posit *judgement* as the 'promised synthesis' or 'solution' to an 'impasse'.[6] Nor should we posit thinking as reflective inaction, willing as non-reflective action and judgement as the reconciliation of reflection and action. Nor should we treat thought as the abstract universal, will as the concrete particular and judgement as the reconciliation of the universal and the particular. No such 'dialectic' or philosophy of reconciliation – in which thinking serves as the thesis, willing as its antithesis and judging as the moment of synthesis – is a road either Arendt or any cosmopolitan thinker would go down.

In reconstructing the absent section on judging, my view is that we should oppose any impulse to elevate judgement as the moment of reconciliation between opposing faculties. To be sure, judgement is an essential component of the life of the modern mind but it serves less as a promised synthesis than as the equivocal source of new repressions and conflicts. What I take from Arendt is that there is *no* faculty of the mind, not even reflective judgement, which does not create as many difficulties as it solves when it enters into the public arena. Judgement without thought is arbitrary; judgement without will is ineffective.[7]

To support this aporetic reading of the text, I shall review in turn Arendt's critiques of the activities of thinking, willing and judging and end on the note of the unity of the life of the mind as a whole.

THE EQUIVOCATIONS OF THINKING

In her report on the Eichmann trial Arendt argued that the most striking quality of Adolf Eichmann, the Nazi official in charge of transporting Jews to the death camps, was his thoughtlessness, his inability to engage in the activity of thinking. The effect of this inability to think, this total absence of thinking, led Arendt to focus on the relationship between thinking and judgement and pose the following question:

> Might the problem of good and evil, our faculty for telling right from wrong, be connected with our faculty for thought? Could the activity of thinking as such, the habit of examining and reflecting upon whatever happens to come to pass, regardless of specific content and quite independent of results, could this activity be of such a nature that it 'conditions' men against evil-doing?
>
> (Arendt 1978b: 1, 5)

Arendt's intuition was that thinking has an internal connection with the ability to judge right from wrong. The final words of her essay on *Thinking and Moral Considerations* express this connection thus:

> The manifestation of the wind of thought is no knowledge; it is the ability to tell right from wrong, beautiful from ugly. And this indeed may prevent catastrophes, at least for myself, in the rare moments when the chips are down.
>
> (Arendt 2003: 189)

Faced with the conjunction of evil-doing and thoughtlessness, Arendt found in the activity of thinking as such an antidote to evil: 'thinking is among the conditions that make men abstain from evil-doing' (Arendt 1978b: 1, 5).

The connection between thinking and judging is formulated by Arendt in basically negative terms: thinking prepares for judgement by purging us of 'fixed habits of thought', 'ossified rules and standards' and 'conventional . . . codes of expression'. As Dana Villa puts it, it creates an 'open space of moral or aesthetic discrimination and discernment' (Villa 1999: 89–90). Arendt characterises judgement as a by-product of the liberating effect of thinking. While thinking deals with the representation of things that are absent, judgement always concerns things close at hand. The liberating effect of thinking is not because it reveals, in the manner of Kantian metaphysics, the truth of what is right: 'We cannot expect', she wrote, 'any moral propositions or commandments, no final code of conduct, from the thinking activity, least of all a new and now allegedly final definition of what is good and what is evil' (Arendt 1978b: 1, 167). Rather she finds something in the 'negative', 'resultless' and 'dissolvent' nature of thinking that, by questioning everything and treating nothing as final, shatters the unreflective morality of good and evil. Arendt draws on metaphors associated with Plato's account of Socrates. Thinking is a 'gadfly' that arouses us from our sleep and makes us feel alive; thinking is a 'midwife' that helps people purge themselves of unexamined prejudices; thinking is an 'electric ray' that momentarily paralyses us, interrupts our activities and infects others with our own perplexities. This capacity to 'stop-and-think' may appear as irritating indecision but at times of crisis, when 'everybody is swept away unthinkingly by what everybody else does and believes in', thinking asserts the claims of inaction – of a refusal to join in. It makes us unsure of what seemed beyond doubt while we were unthinkingly engaged in action. If Eichmann is the representative figure of thoughtlessness, Socrates is the representative figure of the moral efficacy of thinking per se.

This is one side of the picture and it is the more familiar. There is, however, another side to Arendt's analysis of thinking which concerns the danger of *nihilism* inherent in the activity of thinking as such. Arendt acknowledges that thinking 'inevitably has a destructive, undermining effect on all established criteria, values, measurements for good and evil, in short on those customs and rules of conduct we treat of in morals and ethics' (Arendt 1978b: 1, 175). While the strength of thinking lies in its critical capacity, the pathology of thinking is the mirror of its strength. It transforms the non-results of Socratic thinking into negative results. If thinking undermines established notions of piety, it can also turn impiety into its maxim. The spectre of nihilism is latent within the very activity of thinking:

> Thinking can at any moment turn against itself, produce a reversal of old values, and declare these contraries to be 'new values' . . . What we commonly call nihilism . . . is actually a danger inherent in the thinking activity itself. There are no dangerous thoughts; thinking itself is dangerous . . .
>
> (Arendt 1978b: 1, 176)

Since all thought must go through a stage of negating accepted opinions and values, nihilism is the 'ever-present danger of thinking'. While thinking *may* clear the path for judgement, it may equally engender a mere reversal of old values.

We find that thinking has an unexpected affinity with non-thinking. Non-thinking, as Arendt puts it, teaches us only 'to hold fast to whatever the prescribed rules of conduct may be at a given time in a given society' (Arendt 1978b: 1, 177). If the prescribed rules of conduct change and there is a reversal of the basic commandments of Western morality, such as 'Thou shalt not kill' and 'Thou shalt not bear false witness', as there was in the era of totalitarianism, we can as unthinkingly hold to the new code as we did to the old. The ease with such reversals can take place under certain conditions suggested to Arendt that most people were 'fast asleep' when they occurred.

This unexpected affinity of thinking with non-thinking takes up a theme which Arendt referred to in her *The Origins of Totalitarianism* as 'the temporary alliance between the mob and the elite'. There is an alliance, albeit a temporary one, between the atrophy of thinking on the side of the mob and the hypertrophy of thinking on the side of the elite (Arendt 1979: 326–40). The glue that holds this temporary alliance together is nihilism. Arendt drew on Nietzsche's depiction of nihilism in *The Will to Power*: 'What does nihilism mean? That the highest values devaluate themselves. The aim is lacking; "why?" finds no answer' (Nietzsche 1969a: 9). 'Here there is no why', as Primo Levi was to recount the words of an Auschwitz guard. Nietzsche anticipated a time when the values and beliefs taken as the highest manifestation of the spirit of the West would lose their validity and breed a 'spiritless radicalism' full of hostility to culture and images of destruction.

Arendt argued that the barbarism Nietzsche anticipated proved to be a pale image of the barbarism to come. She wrote of the justified disgust with the fake world of bourgeois values felt by the most thoughtful of the 'elite' after the Great War. She wrote of the revulsion felt by radical intellectuals of the front generation over the gulf between the values society espoused and the mechanised murder it actually produced.[8] The intellectual elite became 'absorbed by their desire to see the ruin of this whole world of fake security, fake culture and fake life' and elevated violence, cruelty and destruction as 'supreme capacities of humankind' (Arendt 1979: 330). It turned negativity into nihilism. True, Arendt emphasised the *temporary* nature of the alliance between the elite and the mob, for thinking and thoughtlessness are uneasy bed-fellows, but experience of the pathologies of thinking belies any premature identification of this activity with abstention from evil-doing.

Actually the dangers of thinking are scattered throughout Arendt's writings. Thinking can turn 'what ought to be' into an absolute standard against which everything that exists is treated with indifference or disdain. Thinking can turn the idea of progress into a justification for the most criminal of human actions. Thinking can superimpose the logic of an idea onto the concrete historical process and pretend to know the mysteries of the whole historical process. Thinking can privilege spurious deductions from ideological premises over any activity of understanding or judgement. Heidegger is for Arendt the exemplary case of a philosopher who pushed thinking to the point where its remoteness from the world led to 'error', if not evil – in this case, his engagement with National Socialism (Villa 1997). It is an old story that great philosophers do not necessarily manifest sound political judgement and tend to regard 'with indifference and contempt . . . the world of the city'. Thinking does not only prepare the way for judgement. It *needs* judgement to save itself from itself.

THE EQUIVOCATIONS OF WILLING

Willing for good reason is a less studied section of Arendt's *The Life*

of the Mind. Its long historical passages on philosophical conceptions of the will fail to make transparent what Arendt was trying to
say about this 'faculty'. Arendt was deeply critical of the modern
identification of freedom with the will. Freedom, she insisted, is a
political artefact, not an internal quality of human beings, and its
origins can be traced back to the ancient polis. The faculty of the
will, by contrast, is a modern phenomenon. Its differentiation from
the life of the mind as a whole is the product of modern times:

> We almost automatically equate freedom with free will, that is,
> with a faculty virtually unknown to classical antiquity ... The
> Greeks never became aware of the will as a distinct faculty sepa-
> rate from other human capacities.
>
> (Arendt 1978b: 2, 5)

Arendt argued that the emergence of the will proved to be a
mixed blessing. On the one hand, free will provides the basis of
all modern conceptions of right, morality, responsibility and law-
fulness: 'Without the assumption that the will is free no precept
of a moral, religious or juridical nature could possibly make sense'
(Arendt 1978b: 2, 164). Arendt's own focus, however, is firmly on
the pathologies of willing. For Arendt, the idea of the will is intimately attached to terror rather than to freedom – or to a form of
freedom that can only express itself in the experience of terror.

Arendt's discussion of the Rousseauian doctrine of the 'general
will' in her earlier study *On Revolution* drew the outlines of this connection between terror and the will. She contrasts the idea of the will
which 'essentially excludes all processes of exchange of opinions and
an eventual agreement between them' to the idea of consent with its
'overtones of deliberate choice and considered opinion'. The silent
assumption behind the general will is that the will is an automatic
articulation of interest and that the general will is the articulation
of the national interest. Indivisible and dedicated to unanimity, the
general will can only exist as a singular entity. It conceives of the
people as a 'multiheaded monster, a mass that moves ... as though
possessed by one will'. Its quality is unanimity. It presents itself as
always in the right and it holds not only that the particular opinions
of individuals are subordinate to the whole but that the value of the
individual should be judged by the extent to which 'he acts against

his own interest and against his own will'. The common enemy that unites the nation is not only an external power but the *particular* will of every individual: 'such an enemy existed within the breast of each citizen'. The general will inaugurates a world of mutual suspicion and the abolition of all legal and institutional guarantees. In following Rousseau's dictum that 'it would be absurd for the will to bind itself for the future', it anticipates the structureless quality of totalitarian governments to come: 'Nothing is less permanent and less likely to establish permanence than the will'. Nature itself seems to offer no resistance (Arendt 1988: 73–94). It is not surprising that Arendt presents the faculty of the will as 'the trickiest and the most dangerous of modern concepts and misconceptions' (Arendt 1988: 225).

In *The Life of the Mind* Arendt develops this theme. She found something deeply disturbing in the change in the conception of the future that accompanies the modern concept of progress – 'from that which approaches us to that which we determine by the Will's projects'. There is something frightening in the movement from a political conception of freedom that is possible only in the sphere of human plurality to a philosophical conception of freedom that is fundamentally solipsistic. There is something delusional in the prejudice that political community can represent the will of the people, for all political communities 'constrain the will of their citizens' and at best 'open up some spaces of freedom for action' (Arendt 1978b: 2, 199). Unlike thinking, which manifests itself in internal dialogue, Arendt argued that willing is essentially about domination, not dialogue, even if we are both those who give the orders and those who obey them and take for granted the obedience in ourselves. 'To will is to command', writes Nietzsche, 'inherent in the Will is the commanding thought' (Arendt 1978b: 2, 161). Drawing on Nietzsche, Arendt links the emergence of the will to the sources of evil in the modern world: from the fact that 'the will cannot will backward . . . cannot stop the wheel of time . . . from that impotence Nietzsche derives all human evil' – resentment, thirst for vengeance, the will to power over others (Arendt 1978b: 2, 168). Drawing on Heidegger, Arendt associates the destructiveness of the will with its obsession with the future: 'In order to will the future in the sense of being the future's master, men must forget and finally destroy the past . . .

This destructiveness ultimately relates to everything that is' (Arendt 1978b: 2, 178). Nihilism appears as the natural end of the will:

> Man as he is now, when he is honest, is a nihilist . . . a man who judges of the world as it is that it ought not to be and of the world as it ought to be that it does not exist.
>
> (Arendt 1978b: 2, 169)

Arendt writes of the 'abyss of freedom' that opens up when the will underpins the establishment of a new social order, the 'abyss of nothingness' that opens up before the thought of an absolute beginning, the 'abyss of pure spontaneity' that opens up in the face of the unfounded promises of a final realm of absolute freedom – a realm that 'would indeed spell "the end of all things", a sempiternal peace in which all specifically human activities would wither away' (Arendt 1978b: 2, 207–16). The will, to use a more Hegelian vocabulary, contains the possibility of abstracting from every determination in which it finds itself and of treating every content as a limitation. In such circumstances freedom becomes the 'freedom of the void'. Hegel put it thus: 'Only in destroying something does this negative will have a feeling of its own existence . . . its actualisation can only be the fury of destruction' (Hegel 1991: §5 A and R).[9]

It would appear that for Arendt the spectre of nihilism lies at the margins of thinking but at the core of willing. However, this contrast may be misleading. The source of nihilism lies not in the will as such but in its lack of determinate form. It is the abstraction of the will from its worldly existence that exposes the *abyss* of freedom. Even Arendt cannot in the end separate the achievements of modernity in expanding the space of human freedom from the emergence of the will: our capacity for beginning; our refusal to acknowledge anything not justified in thought; our right of individual personality; our ability to overcome the givenness of the world; even the strength we find in the willing act itself. Not for Arendt, then, the Heideggerian conclusion that to overcome nihilism we need the strength to 'deify the apparent world as the only world' (Arendt 1978b: 2, 168–70). Arendt's final word on the will is *not* one of repudiation or resignation but of 'impasse' – an impasse which, she writes, 'cannot be opened or solved except by an appeal to another mental faculty . . . the faculty of judgment' (Arendt 1978b: 2, 217).

JUDGEMENT AND UNDERSTANDING

Judgement is the ability to apply thinking to particulars or, as Arendt puts it, it is 'the manifestation of thinking in the world' (Arendt 1978b: 1, 193). Arendt follows Kant in distinguishing between *determinate judgement*, which is the capacity to apply given princi-ples established within your own community to any set of particu-lars, and *reflective judgement*, which is the ability to tell right from wrong, beautiful from ugly, without the guidance of fixed rules, that is, 'when all [people] have to guide them is their own judgment' and even when their judgement 'happens to be completely at odds with what they must regard as the unanimous opinion of all those around them' (Arendt 1977b: 294). Determinate judgement is the ancient virtue Aristotle called *phronesis* or prudence, the virtue of the politi-cal actor able to apply generally accepted standards to particular circumstances. Reflective judgement is the capacity for independent judgement which comes to the fore when the world around us goes mad. Arendt wrote of those few individuals who in a totalitarian society were still able to tell right from wrong:

> They went really on their own judgments, and they did so freely; there were no rules to be abided by, under which the particular cases with which they were confronted could be subsumed. They had to decide each instance as it arose, because no rules existed for the unprecedented.
>
> (Arendt 1977b: 295)

Arendt wrote of those Germans who refused complicity with Nazism at great risk to themselves as 'the only ones who dared judge by themselves'. Reflective judgement expresses this capacity to make autonomous judgements irrespective of public opinion, scientific authority or state legislation.

Arendt connects reflective judgement to terms drawn from Kant's *Critique of Judgment* – 'common sense' (*sensus communis*) and 'enlarged mentality'. *Common sense* relates to the world of experience rather than to the mantras of an ideology. It implies the sharing of a common world with others rather than the isolated thinking of an individual and thus breaks the fetters of subjective self-absorption. *Enlarged mentality* is a mindset that pushes beyond the boundaries of any particular mode of perception to behold the world through the eyes of an abstracted generalised other. It seeks to embrace the standpoint of everyone else, to place itself in the shoes of another and see the world from another's standpoint. These connected terms are afforded a distinctly cosmopolitan accent in Arendt's writings:

> One judges always as a member of a community . . . but in the last analysis, one is a member of a world community by the sheer fact of being human; this is one's 'cosmopolitan existence'. When one judges . . . and acts in political matters, one is supposed to take one's bearings from the idea, not the actuality, of being a world citizen.
>
> (Arendt 1992: 75–6)

Arendt addresses the conundrum that we make judgements as members of a particular community. Judgement in this sense is always situated: it does not come from 'nowhere' or from 'on high'. On the other hand, for judgement to be valid, it is not merely an expression of the interests, prejudices or values of our particular community. It must have a universal and timeless validity over and beyond its origins. If judgement is local, it also strives for universality. Arendt translates this striving into political terms. We must judge as members of a *world* community and take our bearings from the idea of being *world* citizens. This basis of judgement is open to everyone by virtue of the sheer fact we are all human beings.

There is reason to think that the distinction between determinate and reflective judgement refers to extremes, neither of which is achievable or even conceivable in practice (Ferrara 1999: 6–7; Makkreel 1994). In the case of determinate judgement the idea of moving non-reflectively from a general principle to a particular judgement obscures the *inescapable* work of interpretation that the actor must engage in. In the case of reflective judgement the idea of judging independently of any social norm obscures our reliance on some community of thought. In their pure forms both determinate and reflective judgements have a mythic quality: one based on the denial of agency and myth of total absorption in the community, the other based on the denial of community and myth of total independence. Judgement always lies between these extremes.

It seems to me that what is at stake in the distinction between determinate and reflective is the relation between the social norms of our immediate national community (in Arendt's example, the norms of Nazi Germany) and the social norms of a more distant yet no less real community, the world community in which we take our bearings from the idea of being world citizens. This is our 'cosmopolitan existence', our human identity, and it is our most vital resource in dark times. Reflective judgement in this account involves above all the capacity for imagination – for re-presenting cosmopolitan standards of judgement which are institutionalised in a variety of forms but which have no visible presence in the society in question. It is along these lines that I would reconstruct the affinity of cosmopolitanism to reflective judgement.

Judgement, however, is not immune to the equivocations and pathologies that beset the other 'faculties' of the mind. The morality of good and evil expresses the danger of nihilism inherent in reflective judgement as such. It is not a question of this or that dangerous judgement but of the dangers of the activity itself of judging. The spectre of nihilism is present since all reflective judgement must go through the stage of discriminating anew between what is good and evil, beautiful and ugly, guilty and innocent.

One of the dangers inherent in the 'faculty' of judgement is that of elevating the moral point of view to supreme status. The 'morality of good and evil', to use Nietzsche's phrase, prioritises morality over all instrumental considerations. It calls for the destruction of evil as the condition for the triumph of the good. Evil is the 'enemy' as the man of *ressentiment* conceives him: 'Here precisely is his deed, his creation: he has conceived "the evil enemy", "the evil one", and this in fact is his basic concept, from which he then evolves, as an afterthought and dependant, a "good one" – himself' (Nietzsche 1969b: 39). In its rush to judgement the morality of good and evil exonerates the 'good' of all responsibility except that of destroying evil. It revels in the 'exultant face-to-face confrontation between Innocence and the Unspeakable Beast' (Finkielkraut 1992: 60). Not only does it make no effort to understand what it judges but it recoils from the task of understanding itself for fear that '*tout comprendre, c'est tout pardonner*'.[10]

The morality of good and evil contrasts sharply with those traditional theodicies dating back to Leibniz, in which the occurrence of evil was an occasion for deep reflection on how human cruelty and misery can co-exist with a just god. Today, it would seem, the judgement of evil can be opposed to all reflection, dialogue or deliberation. The strength of Arendt is to stress from the start the unity of judgement and understanding. She saw the crisis of understanding and crisis of judgement brought about by the rise of totalitarianism so closely inter-twined that she spoke in the same breath of 'the ruin of our categories of thought and standards of judgment'. The essential point, she argued, is to learn to 'understand without preconceived categories and to judge without the set of customary rules which is morality' (Arendt 1992: 388). Judgement and understanding belong to one another.

The relation of judgement to understanding was a key thematic of Arendt's earlier works, collected under the title of *Essays in Understanding*. Understanding has much in common with thinking. Arendt characterises understanding as 'a profoundly *human* activity . . . a specifically human way of being alive; for every single person needs to be reconciled to a world into which he was born a stranger and in which, to the extent of his distinct uniqueness, he always remains a stranger' (Arendt 1992: 308). Understanding is the opposite of indoctrination or ideology. It generates no fixed results. It can only be done in concert with others. It takes into consideration the viewpoints of others. It is prepared to share its conclusions in open and uncoerced discussion with others. It is prepared, like Penelope's weaving, to 'undo every morning what it has finished the night before' (Arendt 1978b: 1, 88). It takes as much pleasure, as Gotthold Lessing put it, in 'making clouds' as it does in clearing them. Understanding differs from thinking in that it relates the subjectivity of thinking to the substance of what is to be understood. Understanding is always of *something*. It must have an object and its task is the comprehension of what exists, not the setting up of an 'ought' which has 'no proper *topos* or place in the world' (Arendt 1978b: 2, 196). It can never be a statement, therefore, only of the subject's opinions, convictions or feelings. This does not imply acquiescence in the arrangements of the world, for the peace understanding established with the world has more warmth in it than this. Nor does it imply empathy with the subjects of our understanding or justification of their actions, for empathy may be unwarranted and justification reveals nothing of subjectivity. The core value of understanding is to preserve the subjective freedom of the individual while at the same time attaching it to the world.[11] This worldliness makes understanding a vital aspect of our cosmopolitan existence (Smith 2007b).

The effects of severing judgement from understanding are mirrored in the effects of severing understanding from judgement. A positivistic social science which excludes moral judgement is one which disables understanding in the face of the extremes of human behaviour (Baehr 2002). It threatens to become scholastic or coldly analytical, incapable of grasping the essence of things. Arendt observes that the tradition of dispassionate and objective analysis in American sociology can make it very difficult to understand what human beings are capable of:

> To describe the concentration camps *sine ira et studio* is not to be 'objective', but to condone them; and such condoning cannot be changed by condemnation which the author may feel duty bound to add but which remains unrelated to the description itself. When I used the image of hell, I did not mean this allegorically but literally . . . In this sense I think that a description of the camps as Hell on earth is more 'objective', that is, more adequate to their essence than statements of a purely sociological or psychological nature.
>
> (Arendt 1992: 404)

In so far as the social sciences try to explain the death camps in terms of political, economic or military utility, they cannot grasp the 'nightmare of reality' before which such scientific categories necessarily fail. Just as moral judgement can be opposed to understanding the world, so too understanding the world can seriously lack judgement.[12] The diremption of understanding and judgement comes full circle when, confronted by our inability to find a *rational*, i.e. utilitarian, explanation for atrocity, we are tempted to declare it beyond human understanding and susceptible *only* to judgement (Lyotard 1988).

The social sciences are reluctant to admit categories of good and evil into their vocabulary. The morality of good and evil rings of theology rather than of science, of tradition rather than modernity, of absolute moral standards rather than cultural relativism, of dogma rather than critical reflection, of one church rather than a plurality of language games, of faith rather than enlightenment. When social scientists address the question of evil, it is to place it within scare quotes: we write not of evil but of conceptions of 'evil' held by social actors and we treat even the conception of 'evil' as the mark of unenlightened consciousness. Ultimately the aim of the social sciences is to dissolve evil – to eliminate it from its own lexicon and from the lexicon of a self-reflexive society. It is difficult, however, to evade the suspicion that the exclusion of the language of evil from the social sciences may serve to conceal its factual existence.

The task of cosmopolitan social theory, as I conceive it, is not to reintroduce the language of evil into the social sciences, still less to justify the flight we now see from the social sciences to a new political theology. However, we do not have to be nostalgic for theodicy to be apprehensive of the effects of spiriting 'evil' away in the name of 'science' and 'technology'. The offence Arendt's critics found in the style of her work on the Eichmann trial – her refusal either to abandon understanding in relation to the perpetrators of the Holocaust or to abandon judgement in relation to the leaders of the Jewish community – may serve as an index of the unity of understanding and judgement that I take to be her prime cosmopolitan virtue.

NIHILISM AND COSMOPOLITANISM

I am aware that my line of argument to some extent goes against the grain of Arendt's own work and her debt to Kant. She seems to believe in the idea of the faculties. She writes, for example, as if thinking and willing are not just two distinct faculties but 'opposites' – one based on the harmonies of internal dialogue, the other on an ongoing conflict between will and counter-will, command and resistance. It appears from this perspective that willing is not only divorced from thinking but prejudicial to it. However, we cannot have a will without thinking. An animal has no will in so far as it does not re-present to itself in thought what it wants. Nor can we think without a will, for thinking itself is an activity. The distinction between thinking and willing is better conceived, following Hegel, as that between a theoretical and practical attitude. These apparently distinct and opposed faculties are in fact inseparable, for both moments can be found in every act of thinking and willing alike.

Arendt also writes as if willing and judging were distinct and opposite faculties. However, she cannot escape the intimate connection between reflective judgement and the exercise of the will. She comments, for instance, that the few Germans who refused to comply with Nazism were the only ones who dared judge for themselves, but we do not know this to be the case. We know only that these individuals had the *courage* to translate their judgement into action – into an act of resistance. They manifested not only a capacity to judge but also the will to resist. Reflective judgement cannot be independent of the will since it can only manifest itself in an act – whether it is the actor who draws general principles from his or her own act of resistance or the observer who stresses the exemplary validity of another's act of resistance.

Arendt, however, often wrote of the *activities* rather than the *faculties* of the mind, and this alternative terminology serves as a caveat for us not to reify the faculties or rationalise their separation. It suggests that human beings do not have distinct *faculties* but rather that we engage in *activities* of thinking, willing, judging, imagining, understanding, etc. and move more or less fluently from one to the other. It also suggests that the philosophical theory of the faculties is an expression of a determinate division of mental and manual labour (Sohn-Rethel 1978) in which the activities of the mind are not only differentiated and specialised but in danger of becoming isolated and fixed.

Arendt's initial question, on the link between thoughtlessness and evil-doing, raises an exceptionally interesting question concerning the role played by the life of the mind in public life. I have extended her thesis by asking whether the proclivity to evil-doing can be explained, in part or in whole, by the division of the life of the modern mind into isolated, distinct and opposing faculties and by the separation of the life of the mind (*vita contemplativa*) from the life of action (*vita activa*). I make use of her conception of 'worldliness' as the cosmopolitan virtue par excellence that refuses to rationalise the division of the life of the mind into reified faculties or its separation from the life of work and politics. The spectre of nihilism is never far from the surface of the life of the modern mind because *worldlessness*, which is akin to subjectivism (Fine 2006a), isolates the mind from the world, gives even to the life of the mind a barbaric and nihilistic aspect. We cannot conceive of cosmopolitanism without the life of the mind but neither can we conceive of it without facing up to the worldlessness that affiliates the life of the mind to the logic of destruction.

CONCLUSION
The elements of a cosmopolitan social theory

Viewed as a whole, this book offers a critical engagement with the modern cosmopolitan tradition, beginning with Kant and then explored through certain key post-war writers, notably Hannah Arendt, Ulrich Beck, Jürgen Habermas and, more broadly, 'the new cosmopolitanism'. The concept of 'cosmopolitanism' has not been addressed in conceptual isolation but through its uses in the language games of social and political thought and its applications to urgent political phenomena: the reforming of social solidarity within the nation-state, the political integration of the European Union, the role of international law in the current world order, the phenomenon of humanitarian military intervention, the prosecution of crimes against humanity, the critique of the life of the modern mind, and the formation of an anti-totalitarian politics. The critical engagement of which I speak has revolved around a number of overlapping thematics and in this conclusion I shall briefly summarise some of the principal ones.

Under the title of taking the 'ism' out of cosmopolitanism, I have argued that in the social sciences cosmopolitanism should be understood as a research agenda rather than a fixed idea or state to be achieved. Cosmopolitanism has its origins in natural law theory and contemporary cosmopolitanism pays its debt, in particular to Kant. I have sought to re-instate cosmopolitanism within the tradition of *social* theory and have used the term 'cosmopolitan social theory' to characterise my own approach and to contrast it with 'the new cosmopolitanism'. I have sought to problematise the tradition of natural law, de-nature the idea of the cosmopolis, extract cosmopolitanism from a teleological philosophy of history and dispel the spectre of a 'cosmopolitan age' to come.

I have addressed the two faces of cosmopolitanism, which I have referred to as the cosmopolitan *outlook* and the cosmopolitan *condition*. By the cosmopolitan outlook I mean a way of seeing the world, a form of consciousness, an emerging paradigm of sociological analysis. It is cosmopolitanism's interpretive moment. By the cosmopolitan condition I refer to an existing social reality, a state of the world, a set of properties belonging to our age. It is cosmopolitanism's external moment. These two aspects of cosmopolitanism are in fact expressions of a unitary phenomenon. On the one hand, the development of cosmopolitan consciousness is itself part of social reality, a vital element of the cosmopolitan condition, and the cosmopolitan vision is itself an intellectual expression of the development of the cosmopolitan condition. On the other hand, the idea of the cosmopolitan condition is itself a mediated, and indeed highly contested, characterisation of the social reality in question. Cosmopolitan being and cosmopolitan consciousness are two sides of the same experience and are reunited through political action.

I have distinguished between three aspects of the cosmopolitan outlook – its theoretical moment (or way of engaging in concept formation in various social scientific disciplines); its empirical moment (or way of understanding the social phenomena of the modern age); and its normative moment (or way of judging what people do). I have argued that in all three respects – theoretical, empirical and normative – cosmopolitanism is a form of radicalism that challenges the status quo. It confronts the boundedness of the methodological approaches of the social sciences not least through its critique of 'methodological nationalism'. It refuses to accept the restricted understanding of our age in terms of essentialising particularisms (e.g. Germanness, Britishness, Jewishness) but rather explains national peculiarities through the general structural developments of modernity and the inter-subjective relations in which these particulars are inserted. It resists the reduction of either politics or science to a moral point of view that demonises the Other as it idealises the Self.

I have argued that cosmopolitan categories of understanding and standards of judgement pose a challenge both to the *modernist* identification of the universal with some socially selected particular (for instance, the identification of the 'universal class' or the 'universal nation' with the interests and values of humanity as a whole), and to the *postmodern* identification of universalism as such with the suppression of difference and exclusion of the Other. Cosmopolitan social theory casts a critical eye on the modernist politics of orthodox socialism and nationalism and on postmodernist 'identity' politics. It has the virtue today of facing up to the decline of the 'old left', with its fixation on the politics of anti-imperialism regardless of substantive content, and the decline of the 'new left' with its own fixation on particular visible identities regardless of our common human condition (Postone 2006).

I have not tried to formulate the cosmopolitan outlook in a neat phrase. It does not, and certainly should not in my view, idealise the age in which we live. Rather it interrogates the foundations of critical theory by breaking down the assumptions both of what has been called a 'homologising logic' (Caverero 1992), in which differences are erased and subsumed to a far from innocent uniform standard, and of ethical conformity to visible identities. At the same time it ties its own negativity to an ethical universalism (Oliver 1993: 1). It takes off from the understanding that every individual is more than what society gives them and that no one actually coincides with what the sociologists call their social 'identity' (Gorz 1989: 176). The 'moreness' to which I refer is our humanity and cosmopolitanism occupies the space between our humanity as such and our 'local' identities.

I have drawn from Beck and the new cosmopolitanism the insight that cosmopolitanism does not expect that in the era of global interconnections people will or should live 'without local, immediate, concrete or exclusive bonds', as one critic has put it, or that 'in a borderless society of strangers . . . the distinction between local and strangers, locals and cosmopolitans, friends and enemies, civilisation and barbarism, the West and the Rest is abolished' (Ossewaarde

2007: 384). However, to quote again the same critic, it does indeed invite each human being to become 'friends of humanity'. I have argued that what it means to become a friend of humanity is itself socially situated and very much depends on our local position.

I have argued that the concept of the 'cosmopolitan condition' refers to the development not only of certain forms of cosmopolitan consciousness but also of certain laws, institutions and practices. There is a sense in which the cosmopolitan condition is 'out there' in the world. We can try to *understand* what it is, and there is indeed much disagreement over how it is to be understood, but we cannot *determine* what it is. In this regard cosmopolitanism is not just an abstract ideal, but an evolving set of social forms which, like all social forms, is a potential object of confirmation or criticism, reform or repudiation. It can neither simply be willed into being nor willed away. Since the cosmopolitan condition is constructed through the activities of humankind, it can be reconstructed and deconstructed, is always unfolding, and may or may not accord with our own sense of what is right.

I have maintained, following Habermas, that the cosmopolitan condition is a *complex* social reality. It incorporates what I take to be three separate moments or elements: first, the development of a variety of new practices, institutions and laws in the sphere of interstate relations; second, the refraction of these new practices, institutions and laws on all preceding fields of right and law (including those of the nation-state, civil society, the family, morality, civil and political rights and private property); and third, the recalibration of the 'system of right' as a whole in the light of these new developments. I have viewed cosmopolitanism more like a modern cathedral than an ancient temple, more like the fluid and adaptive organism of a human brain than a simple relation between structure and function, more like a set of flows between nodal points than a fixed state of affairs. It is not identical to any particular institution (such as the UN, a world parliament, international law, human rights, international courts, global civil society), but to an open, conflictual and dynamic system in which the relation between form and function is always relative to its place within the system as a whole.

I have maintained that there is a sense in which the cosmopolitan condition may be viewed as a *necessary* stage in the development of the idea of right – necessary in the same sense that the development of money out of generalised commodity production is necessary, or the development of capital out of generalised money relations is necessary, or the development of civil society out of independent private property and the development of the nation-state out of civil society are necessary. I do not mean that history has to follow this particular path of progression. There are many societies in which – for various historical reasons – money, capital, civil society or the nation-state failed to develop organically or were stopped from developing by external forces. Looking backwards, however, we can reconstruct the *logic* by which a movement (from value to money to capital in the economic system and from right to civil society to the state in the legal system) occurs in the absence of exogenous inhibiting factors. From this perspective I have treated the advent of cosmopolitanism not merely as a contingent happenstance but as the product of the complex web of interrelations between discrete societies. Thus it may be acknowledged that, while we do not live in a cosmopolitan age, there is a sense in which we may be said to live in an age of cosmopolitanism.

I have formulated the cosmopolitan condition as a stage of development in the *system* of right. Drawn from Hegel, my conception of a 'system' does not hold that the system of right is based on natural presuppositions, or that it is without an environment beyond itself, or that it is closed and non-conflictual, or that cosmopolitanism represents its final synthesis. On the contrary, I have argued that the cosmopolitan condition is to be conceived as a *social* system; that it is in constant movement, torn asunder by conflicts, strains and contradictions; that it can only exist in relation to its economic environment; and that the emergence of cosmopolitan social forms should be conceived as a kind of sublation which reproduces as well as overcomes all prior conflicts. The integration of the cosmopolitan condition should be seen as a problem whose solution is always provisional, precarious and tentative (Chernilo 2007a). Movement, metamorphosis, tension and crisis are its key characteristics. Among the internal conflicts of cosmopolitanism I have addressed those which arise between criteria of peace, human rights and global governance; between its normative and analytical applications; between the different levels of the cosmopolitan condition; between the universal and the particular, the global and the local.

I see two poles of misunderstanding the cosmopolitan

condition. The positive pole of misunderstanding has an affinity to natural law theory. In its idealised view of the cosmopolitan condition, cosmopolitanism appears as the apex of modernity and culmination of the idea of right as such. It is based on natural or rational presuppositions and presented as the end of history. It idealises the cosmopolitan condition either by singling out one of its moments for special treatment (human rights, international law, the UN, international criminal courts, etc.) or by harmonising the idea of the whole (including the layers of post-national, transnational and international citizenship). Cosmopolitanism appears here as the moment of synthesis or reconciliation overcoming all previous divisions and conflicts.

The negative pole is to say either that cosmopolitanism does not exist – that what is called the cosmopolitan condition is the wrong name for the sovereign exercise of state power aided by the denial of sovereignty to weaker state powers – or that it does exist in the sense that it marks a new stage in social evolution but that it presents itself as a system of freedom when in actuality it is a system of imperialism, domination and violence. These negative viewpoints, based on the re-assertion in one case of the doctrine of the state and in the other of the ontology of violence, are often fused in the critique of cosmopolitanism as the continuation of old power politics and as the expression of a new imperialism. I have declared my wariness of the doctrine of 'anti-cosmopolitanism' not only because of its scurrilous history but also because of its sometimes current conceptual shortcomings.

I have argued that these interpretative poles are more closely interlocked than they appear at first sight, that idealisation and disillusionment are two sides of the same medal. Thus the representation of international law as the answer to all the problems facing political and social theory is closely tied to the disillusionment that arises when international law fails to perform its allotted role. If it is true that an idealised cosmopolitanism can treat the law as its *deus ex machina*, it is equally the case that critics of cosmopolitanism can base their scepticism towards human rights on the failure of human rights to live up to an ideal which exists basically inside their own heads.[1] The law only appears as nothing from the perspective of one who treats it as everything. The cosmopolitan call for an international court of law, with international armies at its disposal, capable of making judgements based exclusively on the pursuit of justice, may not be able to explain how they can avoid becoming either an imperial court or a tool in the plans of a great power, but this, after all, is the stuff of politics. Let us imagine a scenario in which the leaders of the powers which have invaded Iraq and the leaders of the 'Resistance' which have blown up fellow citizens as a strategy of resistance have to face public judgement before an international court of law. It may not solve anything but it opens up interesting possibilities.

My own approach to cosmopolitan social theory may be illustrated through its conception of human rights. I have proposed that human rights are a *contradictory and relative social form*. *Contradictory* because of the gap between the universality of the concept and its particular instantiation – between the freedom, equality and solidarity the concept promises and the dependence, class division and moral indifference its existence also contains. *Relative* because human rights are a finite achievement in relation to all other rights – be they the rights of property, rights of moral conscience, rights of association in civil society or rights of political participation in the nation-state – and they should not be turned into a new kind of absolute. *Social* because human rights are a historical achievement of the modern age (the concept of 'human rights' arose during the Second World War), albeit a precarious and ever threatened achievement, and neither an artefact of nature (as is imagined by natural law theory) nor a mere construction of the state (as is imagined in legal positivism). Finally human rights are a *form* because all rights, human rights included, express the various forms and shapes of subjectivity which prevail in contemporary capitalist society.

I have maintained that rights should be understood as a social form of the subject in the modern world. It expresses one aspect of our complex relations to other subjects. If we consider modernity as a *system of rights*, as Kant and Hegel sought to do, in which individual right, morality, civil society and the state are key fields of contestation and struggle, *human rights* are the product of a certain stage of the historical development of international society – of postnational federations, transnational civil society, global public spheres, international law and human rights conventions. Human rights share all the contradictions of the rights that precede them and mean nothing without the power of coercion to enforce them. There is much conceptual slippage in the literature, as when crimes against humanity are understood as a serious violation of human rights rather than of international criminal law, or when human rights are equated with the right to have rights in general rather than with a specific subset of rights; but to remedy such slippages is the task of a science of right.

I have attempted to distinguish between the critique of human rights and the mere dismissal of the idea of right. A standard criticism of the institution of human rights is that it contributes little to the struggle against capitalist exploitation and political domination; that its promotion by humanitarians turns it into a palliative that may be useful for a limited protection of individuals but blunts political resistance; and that it expands the imperial writ until it reaches the end-state of empire. Such criticism warns against the depoliticising trap of human rights and draws a strict division between the top-down employment of human rights as an instrument of control and the bottom-up employment of human rights as a redemptive and emancipatory instrument of resistance. It purports to defend politics against 'preachers of moralism, suffering humanity and humanitarian philanthropy' (Douzinas 2007: 293). Against such airy polemics, I have argued that everything interesting occurs in the in-between.[2] In any event, it makes little sense to separate these two moments as distinct modalities – one redemptive and the other imperialistic – as if struggle and institutionalisation were not both endemic in the idea of human rights itself.

I have defended the idea of humanity as a social accomplishment of the modern age and expressed a wariness of critics who write with scorn of 'humanity' and 'humanitarianism' as if these terms are necessarily opposed to political action. While the politics of human rights can of course downplay politics in favour of law, there is nothing inherently depoliticising in the turn to law. I am wary of constructing a sharp divide between 'actually existing cosmopolitanism' and the 'cosmopolitanism to come'. In this diremption all ethics, spirit and hope are placed on the side of the 'to come' and all law, naivety, domination and deception are placed on the side of the 'actually existing'. The appeal of this diremption forgets that in both cases we are speaking of cosmopolitanism; there must be some family resemblance between them, or our use of the same term in both cases is merely rhetorical. The forced separation of the good and bad sides of cosmopolitanism reminds me of a pre-critical methodology – akin, perhaps, to that of Proudhon's forced separation of the good and bad sides of private property. The point, as I have sought to demonstrate, is to explore the phenomenon itself, in its actuality, not take what we like and call it our heritage and discard the rest as the detritus of history.[3]

What is at stake in cosmopolitan social theory is our relation to the natural law framework in which the concept of cosmopolitanism was formed and from which it is now seeking to emancipate itself. The history of cosmopolitanism has traversed various stages of natural law theory: traditional natural law, modern natural law, postnational natural law and now postmodern natural law. The difficult task is not to dispose of the idealisations of natural law theory but to retain its rational kernel while drawing cosmopolitanism firmly into the terrain of history, politics and the social. This is as much the terrain of wars between nation-states, the slaughter of civilians, the break up of empires, the rise of imperialism and nationalism, the emergence of totalitarian movements, global market forces, ethnic nationalism, religious fundamentalism and bloody forms of anti-imperialism as it is of the gentler virtues. It is on this terrain that cosmopolitanism seeks to establish its own ethical and critical space.

These are my thematics. There are of course many fruitful areas of cosmopolitan thinking that I have not explored in this short book. This book is offered as an invitation to enjoy what is being done within this roughly defined research agenda and to participate in the difficult and obstacle-strewn task of thinking, writing and researching in a cosmopolitan way. That the coinage of cosmopolitanism may from time to time be debased does not diminish its value.

NOTES

1 Taking the 'ism' out of cosmopolitanism

1 The underlying logic has some resemblance, though surely not in accord with Beck's own wishes, to a dialectic in which the 'thesis' appears as the traditional unity of morality and politics prior to the Treaty of Westphalia, the 'antithesis' is the modern diremption of morality and politics after the Treaty of Westphalia, and the 'synthesis' is the reunification of morality and politics under a cosmopolitan register. This formulaic philosophy of history renders invisible the troubled history of nation-states throughout the modern age and the equally troubled history of social scientific attempts to understand and intervene in this history.

2 Durkheim was not alone in seeing the Great War as a clash of civilisations and a contest of rival 'national' values and virtues. Exchanges of fire on the battlefields took place alongside a war of ideas in which the big intellectual and spiritual cannons blazed with accusations, denials and counter-accusations. French intellectuals of all backgrounds and persuasions were united in the belief that the war was between civilisation and barbarism, a view confirmed by the catalogue of German atrocities and oppressions on and off the battlefield, and that France had a universal mission on behalf of humankind. Durkheim certainly had an appropriate target in Treitschke who was openly antisemitic.

3 Beck criticises the sociological tradition for falsely universalising particular national experiences. He put the matter thus: 'There is an inner affinity between the national and universal perspectives. One's own society serves as the model for society in general, from which it follows that the basic characteristics of universal society can be derived from an analysis of *this* society' (Beck 2006a: 28). This may be a recognisable trait of sociology but so too is understanding other cultures and paying careful attention to their own truth claims and value judgements (Taylor 1994).

4 Again there is a certain resemblance between the logic of Beck's argument and a philosophy of history in which the 'thesis' is humanistic universalism, the 'antithesis' is methodological nationalism and the 'synthesis' is cosmopolitanism.

5 The new cosmopolitanism has an equivocal relation to the two cornerstones of the self-understanding of modern societies, nationalism and socialism (Chernilo and Fine 2003). The core deficiency it sees in these great intellectual and political movements of the modern age is that they prioritise the particular interests and values of a nation or class *over* the universal interests of humanity or identify these particular interests and values *with* those of humanity as a whole. The shibboleth

it seeks to overcome is the idea of a 'universal' class or nation whose particular values and interests are identified with the general interests of humanity as a whole. The new cosmopolitanism also parts company with the practice, if not idea, of internationalism, seeing in it an ideology deployed by national elites to justify the universality of their own particular interests. At one time, to be a good internationalist one had only to support the Soviet Union through all its twists and turns of its foreign policy (Fine 1990; Hobsbawm 1994; Rodinson 1972). Against these competing forms of particularism and the spurious universals they generate, the new cosmopolitanism presents itself as a collective endeavour to reconstruct a *genuine* universalistic outlook and overcome the narrow particularism and merely abstract universalism constitutive of the modern political imagination. It wishes to build a radically different vision: one which no longer looks to a particular class or nation as the embodiment of universal values, still less to the destruction of another class or nation as the condition of human emancipation, but to the construction of a complex, differentiated, lawful and institutionalised universalism different from all these spurious forms of reconciliation.

6 The tension between liberalism and the megalomania of the state is already immanent within Hobbes's conception of the Leviathan. In the state of nature people are driven by 'fear of death' and 'desire for security' into 'seeking peace'. Reason demands a renunciation of their natural liberty and the erection of a 'common power', a 'mortal God', to compel the performance of promises and obedience to laws. This common power reduces the plurality of voices into one will, so that everyone must 'own and acknowledge himself to be the author of whatsoever he that so beareth their person, shall act or cause to be acted in those things which concern the common peace and safety' (Hobbes 1996: 122). The sovereign 'can do no injury to any of his subjects nor ought he to be by any of them accused of injustice' (Hobbes 1996: 124).

2 Confronting reputations

1 Kant's key essays are: 'Idea for a Universal History from a Cosmopolitan Point of View' (1785), 'Reviews of Herder's *Ideas on the Philosophy of the History of Mankind*' (1784–5); 'On the common saying "This may be true in theory but it does not apply in practice"' (1793), 'Toward Perpetual Peace: A Philosophical Sketch' (1795–6), 'International Right' in *The Metaphysics of Morals* (1797); and 'The contest of the faculties' (1798). They are collected in Kant 1991.

2 In *The Rights of Others* Seyla Benhabib elaborates thus the idea of cosmopolitan right: 'A cosmopolitan theory of justice cannot be restricted to schemes of *just* distribution on a global scale, but must also incorporate a vision of *just* membership. Such just membership entails: recognizing the moral claim of refugees and asylees to *first* admittance;

a regime of porous borders for immigrants; an injunction against denationalization and the loss of citizens rights; and the vindication of the right of every human being "to have rights", that is, to be a *legal* person, entitled to certain inalienable rights, regardless of the status of their political membership' (Benhabib 2004: 3).

3 The immediate occasion for Kant's writing of *Perpetual Peace* was an event that was hardly predisposed to the cosmopolitan idea: it was the signing of the Treaty of Basel in which Prussia agreed to hand over to France all territories west of the Rhine in exchange for being allowed to join Russia and Austria in the east in partitioning Poland. This was the sort of *realpolitik* treaty that Kant condemned as a mere 'suspension of hostilities' and as the opposite of true peace (Reiss 1991).

4 The first three articles of the 1789 *Declaration of the Rights of Man and Citizen* illustrate the tension succinctly: 'Article I. Men are born and remain free and equal of right; social distinctions may be founded only on the common usefulness. Article II. The aim of any political association is to preserve the natural and inalienable rights of man; these are the rights liberty, property, security, and resistance to oppression. Article III. The principle of all sovereignty lies essentially in the nation; no group, no individual may have any authority that does not expressly proceed from it.' These articles articulate three key republican principles: rights belong equally to all individuals as such; the aim of the state is to give political support for these rights; no one can claim rights that the nation or people has not authorised. That the free and equal man is the citizen is made explicit in Article VI of the *Declaration*: 'The law is the expression of the general will; all citizens have the right to work towards its creation; it must be the same for all, whether it protects or punishes.'

5 It was true that the scope of legitimate war was expanded to the point where 'there was hardly anyone against whom war could not be undertaken'; that it was left to the judgement of individual states to decide how far they could safely refrain from the forcible prosecution of their rights; that the majority of nations sought only to strengthen themselves at the expense of others and the good faith of nations was always a subject of suspicion among other nations; and that there was little prospect of 'a human legislative power of universal character and world-wide extent' (Bull 1992, 1995; Tuck 2001).

6 Kant showed he was aware that existing interstate relations were not exactly like a Hobbesian state of nature, when he acknowledged that they already contained *some* idea of right. As Katrin Flikschuh has argued, 'the strict dichotomy between 'natural condition' and 'civil condition' disappears and is replaced by the distinction between 'provisional Right' and 'preremptory Right' (Flikschuh 2000: 176). At the level of the individual state, Kant envisaged the transformation of provisional into preremptory right as a process of reform in which the obligation of individuals to enter into a civil condition *under* the legal authority of the state is turned into a social and political reality. At the

international level he envisaged an equally gradual transformation of provisional into preremptory right that would eventually encompass the whole Earth.

7 The relation of Kant to the tradition of natural law seems more like an ongoing dialogue than a sudden rupture. Stephen Toulmin recounts how central the Greek word 'cosmopolis' was to this natural law tradition. It had the connotation of bringing together the *cosmos* (order of nature) and the *polis* (order of human society). It expressed an idea of harmony in which the structure of nature would reinforce a rational social order and human affairs would proceed in step with heavenly affairs (Toulmin 1992: 67). For *traditional* natural law theory this meant that what God is to nature, so too the king is to the state, the husband to his wife and the father to his family (Toulmin 1992: 128). *Modern* natural law tradition, culminating in Kant, was a movement to rationalise the relation between natural and social order. Kant added a further political dimension to the cosmopolis but his conception of 'universal cosmopolitan existence' as the highest purpose of nature was in tune with the well-established principles of natural law theory. The language Kant used conveys the enthusiasm of discovery. He refers to the formation of a federation of peoples or nations as a 'sublime idea' and one which brings the legal constitution of humankind near to its 'greatest possible perfection'. In line with the presuppositions of natural law theory the institution of an external authority appears to Kant as the dividing line between the state of nature and civil society at the international level.

8 Hegel noted that in the wars of coalition waged by England against France, 'the entire people has pressed for war on several occasions and has in a sense compelled the ministers to wage it . . . Only later when emotions had cooled, did people realise that the war was useless and unnecessary and that it had been entered into without calculating the cost' (Hegel 1991: §329A).

9 Discipline makes for highly effective fighting forces. Hegel comments, for instance, that 'In India, five hundred men defeated twenty thousand who were not cowards, but who simply lacked the disposition to act in close association with others' (Hegel 1991: §327A).

10 Ironically the young Marx's critique of Hegel's Doctrine of the State in the *Philosophy of Right* follows closely the lines of Hegel's original critique of Kant.

3 Cosmopolitanism and political community

1 This chapter draws in part on Fine (1994a) and Fine and Smith (2003). I am grateful to William Smith for permission to use some of our joint work.

2 The idea of 'constitutional patriotism' was originally developed by Dolf Sternberger in the 1960s. He associated it with the tradition of eighteenth-century republicanism, prior to the emergence of modern

nationalism, and presented it in post-war West Germany as a functional equivalent to conventional notions of national belonging. He also sought to divest patriotism of its traditional connotations of self-sacrifice for *la patrie* (Rosales 2001; Turner 2004: 297).

3 William Smith observes that the ambivalences of constitutionalism are reflected in the work of Hannah Arendt. In *On Revolution* and her essay on 'Civil Disobedience' she discusses the conservative character of law and judicial institutions whilst at the same time celebrating the US Constitution as a revisable mechanism that underpins the durability and structure of the body politic. (Smith 2007c)

4 Chernilo argues that Habermas's method, concepts and normative standpoints have always been compatible with a broadly cosmopolitan agenda. The fact that he now explicitly uses the term 'cosmopolitanism' may be down to a number of reasons, but his overall theoretical project has always been cosmopolitan-friendly (Chernilo 2008b).

4 Cosmopolitanism and international law

1 This chapter draws in part on Smith and Fine (2004). I am grateful to William Smith for permission to use some of our joint work.

2 The distinction Habermas makes between traditional and post-traditional forms of civil society is central to the critique of civil society romanticism. In its traditional form civil society refers to longstanding communities (ethnic, religious, patriarchal, etc.) whose historical depth may make them resistant to modern political and economic forces but whose normative deficiency is indicated by their lack of space for individual choice or critical reflection. Post-traditional civil society is an arena of association in which emphasis is placed on choosing those with whom we associate and choosing the terms on which associations are formed. In place of a conventional orientation to fixed rules, unreflective duty and respect for authority, this modern form of civil society requires a mature self-consciousness through which individuals learn to evaluate moral authority in terms of general ethical maxims. Civil society is in this sense a 'life-world', a site of mutual understanding and common convictions in which speaker and hearer meet, reciprocally raise claims about the world, criticise or confirm these validity claims, and try to settle their disagreements.

3 Habermas's claim that 'normative agreement concerning human rights . . . is a matter of dispute between the West . . . and Asians and Africans' and must be the subject of international dialogue may be less justified than it might appear (Habermas 1999b: 184–5). Although on some issues some states express disagreements in terms of interpretive declarations and reservations, there is a prevailing consensus over human rights norms. What strikes the social theorist about human rights law is how rich and diverse it is and how little sign there is of dissensus over principles, even if there is some conflict over the interpretation of principles – for example, in relation to current US interpretations of torture.

4 I am thinking in part of the UN's interventions in Congo in the 1960s, Somalia, Cambodia, Rwanda and Bosnia in the 1990s, many of which failed but nonetheless offer a sobering reminder of why we need an international organisation. I am also thinking of the many UN sub-groups – UNESCO, UNICEF, WHO, UNRWA, UNHCR, UNCTAD, ICTY, ICC, etc. – which tend to do the 'soft' and routine tasks of international regulation and assistance.

5 It reveals, for instance, the one-sidedness of the 'American' argument that there is something deeply problematic about international law simply because of its lack of democratic legitimacy; for this draws a misleading parallel between constitutionalism at national and international levels. It also reveals the one-sidedness of the 'European' claim for the legitimacy of international law based exclusively on the substantive ground of its protection of human rights and the fair outcomes this generates.

6 Reference to the history of US commitment to an internationalist strategy has an element of truth to it. We only have to think of the impetus President Wilson gave to the formation of the League of Nations and the Kellogg-Briand Pact (proscribing wars of aggression) after the First World War and the establishment of the Nuremberg Charter and Tribunal, the UN and the Universal Declaration of Human Rights after the Second World War. Eleanor Roosevelt famously wrote in 1948: 'Taken as a whole, the Delegation of the United States believes that this a good document – even a great document – and we propose to give it our full support. [...] This Universal Declaration of Human Rights may well become the international Magna Carta of all men everywhere.' Even Ronald Reagan was moved to say in 1989 that 'For people of good will around the world, that document is more than just words: It's a global testament of humanity, a standard by which any humble person on Earth can stand in judgement of any government on Earth' (http://en.wikipedia.org/wiki/Universal_Declaration_of_Human_Rights). Talcott Parsons, observing that the US involvement in the Second World War was a break from the isolationism that had often marked its history, pushed hard for more vigorous and international law-abiding US involvement in the world scene.

7 Consider Hannah Arendt's citation of Montesquieu's insight in *On Revolution*: 'only power arrests power'.

5 Cosmopolitanism and humanitarian military intervention

1 This paper arises out of joint research with William Smith. I am extremely grateful for his generous and wise collaboration. Our research was funded by the ESRC New Securities Programme, directed by Stuart Croft, and I am grateful to the ESRC for its support.

2 The virtue of Habermas's approach lies in the concreteness of his judgement and his own readiness to make a decision in the face of

ambivalence. We may or may not agree with his judgements but he does not shy away from making them. We may question, for example, the legitimacy of the contrast he draws between Anglo-American uni-lateralism and European multilateralism, but we know where he stands. There is an interesting contrast in this respect between Habermas and Derrida. In his dialogue with Habermas on *Philosophy in Terror* Derrida also looks on the violence of the world through a cosmopolitan gaze. He at once expresses support for the establishment of a UN army as an effective intervening force and articulates his own equivocation over this proposal:

> I am not unaware of the utopic character of the horizon I'm sketching out here, that of an international institution of law and an international court of justice with their own autonomous force … this unity of force and law is not only utopic but aporetic … we would be reconstituting a new figure … of universal sovereignty, of absolute law with an effective autonomous force at its disposal.
>
> (Habermas and Derrida 2003a: 114–15)

Ambivalence punctuates every dot and comma of Derrida's text:

> The Progress of cosmopolitanism, yes … But cosmopolitanism … presupposes some form of state sovereignty, something like a world state … The state is … at once remedy and poison.
>
> (Habermas and Derrida 2003a: 123–33)

I am less convinced than Derrida that we should pin our faith on the building of a UN army or that we can simply declare our ambivalence in general philosophical terms. Cosmopolitanism must be able to draw upon the resource of political actors capable of making complex and informed judgements on urgent questions of public deliberation. It has to *grapple* with ambivalence.

We seem to be increasingly haunted by the spectre of terrorism: images of 9/11 and 7/7, images of the beheading of hostages, images of the suicide bombing of many innocent civilians by the 'resistance' in Iraq. On the surface, much of this terrorism appears to have lost all rational connection with political instrumentality and appears distinct from the traditional terrorism that has marked national movements in, say, Algeria or Ireland, or even in Israel/Palestine. On the other side, it may well be the case that under current American leadership much of what is called the 'war on terror' works to 'regenerate the causes of the evil they claim to eradicate' (Habermas and Derrida 2003a: 100). The cosmopolitan outlook is a refusal to lose our sense of astonishment in the face of either form of violence and an understanding that we are not defenceless. In seeking an alternative to the ill-defined 'war on terror', it declares that international law must be respected and made effective. In resisting terrorism, it reminds us that 'those called "terrorists" are not in this context "others" whom we as "Westerners" can no longer understand. We must not forget that they were often recruited, trained, and even armed, and for a long time, in various Western ways by a Western world that itself . . . invented the word, the techniques and the politics of "terrorism"' (Habermas and Derrida 2003a: 115).

Law and politics are the two sides of the cosmopolitan coin: they bring together institution and outlook, judgement and understanding. Were judgement split from understanding, law might revert to demonisation of the perpetrators. Conversely, were understanding split from judgement, politics might revert to mere justification of the perpetrators. The function of international law is not to demonise those who commit crimes but to hold them responsible for their actions and thereby to humanise them. The function of political understanding is not to justify the crimes such perpetrators commit – whether in the name of other crimes committed by the West or of higher motives projected onto the perpetrators themselves – but to confront the politics of subjectivity that celebrates terrorism as the method of choice.

6 Cosmopolitanism and punishment

1 I am thinking of intellectuals such as Albert Camus, Raymond Aron, Arthur Koestler and Hannah Arendt herself, and civil society group-ings like the Bertrand Russell Tribunal. This tribunal was designed to investigate and publicise war crimes by American forces and its allies during the Vietnam War. It was constituted in November 1966 and conducted two sessions in 1967. Representatives of eighteen coun-tries participated in the tribunal, which called itself the International War Crimes Tribunal. More than thirty individuals testified or provided information, among whom were military personnel from the United States and both sides in Vietnam (http://en.wikipedia.org/wiki/Russell_Tribunal).

2 In the 1963 Auschwitz trials in Frankfurt the West German authorities decided to use domestic rather than international law to handle the prosecution of personnel from the extermination camp. The leading prosecutor, Fritz Bauer, urged Germans 'to understand their inner responsibility and not take the easy way out'. The defendants were accused of murder and to secure conviction the prosecution had to prove not that they were merely carrying out orders but that they were sadists who killed at whim and on their own individual initia-tive. The resulting press coverage turned into what Wittman called a 'pornography of the Holocaust' and allowed ordinary Germans to distance themselves from the crimes on display. Arendt points out in her account of the trial that the defence was based on the little-man theory that 'the defendants had been forced to do what they did and

were in no position to know that it was criminally wrong' and that 'the selections of able-bodied people on the ramp had in effect been a rescue operation because otherwise "all those coming in would have been exterminated"' (Arendt 2003: 237). Arendt concluded that only when Judge Hofmeyer pronounced the sentences did one realise how much 'damage to justice' was done by not taking into account the everyday reality of Auschwitz.

3 We may hear in this reductive view of history an echo of Goebbels' comment, 'we will go down in history as the greatest statesmen of all times or as their greatest criminals', or as Eichmann's lawyer put it, 'you are decorated if you win and go to the gallows if you lose'.

4 Alain Finkielkraut argues ambiguously that the Holocaust was 'from Eichmann to the engineers on the trains ... a crime of employees' and that it was 'precisely to remove from *crime* the excuse of *service* and to restore the quality of *killers* to law-abiding citizens ... that the category of "crimes against humanity" was formulated' (Finkielkraut 1992: 3–4). Zygmunt Bauman adopts a mechanistic view both of sociology and of the actual workings of bureaucracy with less equivocation (Bauman 1990). For a critique of Bauman's approach to the question of responsibility, see Fine and Hirsh (2000).

5 This theme is taken up by Primo Levi who, in *The Periodic Table*, describes the SS as 'ordinary men' and in *If This is a Man* argues that save for exceptions, they were not monsters but 'average human beings' who had been 'reared badly' and 'subjected to a terrifying miseducation' (Levi 1995).

6 In her essay on 'Fascism and representation', Gillian Rose used the label 'Holocaust piety' to characterise this way of thinking: 'It is this reference to the "ineffable" that I would dub "Holocaust piety" ... The "ineffable" is invoked by a now widespread tradition of reflection on the Holocaust: by Adorno, by Holocaust theology, Christian and Jewish, more recently by Lyotard, and now by Habermas. According to this view, "Auschwitz" or "the Holocaust" are emblems for the breakdown in divine and/or human history. The uniqueness of this break delegitimises names and narratives as such, and hence all aesthetic or apprehensive representation ... the search for a decent response to those brutally destroyed is conflated with the quite different response called for in the face of the inhuman capacity for such destruction. To argue for silence, prayer, the banishment equally of poetry and knowledge, in short, the witness of "ineffability", that is, non-representability, is to *mystify what we dare not understand*, because we fear that it may be all too understandable, all too continuous with what we are – human, all too human' (Rose 1996: 41–3).

7 The philosopher, Jean-François Lyotard, compared the Holocaust with an earthquake so catastrophic as to 'destroy not only lives, buildings, and objects but also the instruments used to measure earthquakes directly and indirectly' (Lyotard 1988: 56). In his thought experiment he imagined a situation in which not only vast numbers are extermi-

nated but the means to prove this happened are also destroyed and the authority of the tribunal supposed to establish the crime is discredited on the ground that the judge is 'merely a criminal more fortunate than the defendant in war'. There are parallels between the questions Lyotard and Arendt pose but this should not be allowed to obscure the opposing answers they give and the different sensibilities which inform them.

7 Cosmopolitanism and the life of the mind

1 This chapter is based on an original paper written for *Philosophy and Social Criticism* (2007). I wish to give special thanks to Alessandro Ferrara for inviting me to contribute to this volume and for his encouragement and insight.

2 See 'The Crisis in Culture: Its Social and its Political Significance', 'Truth and Politics' and 'Freedom and Politics' in Arendt (1977b), especially pp. 219–26.

3 Beiner and Nedelsky (2001: 165). Other key texts on Arendt's approach to judgement include: Beiner (1983: ch. 6), d'Entrèves (2000) Beiner (1994) and Beiner in Arendt (1992).

4 An analogy might be drawn here with Marx scholarship. When Marx scholars sought to reconstruct Marx's planned but incomplete work on law, morality and the state, a less than satisfactory approach was simply to pull together the various passages in which Marx commented on or expressed his opinions about these various issues. The more fruitful and certainly more scientific approach was to reconstruct the methodology that Marx employed in his critique of political economy and apply it, flexibly and with due regard to the shift of subject matter, to the absent critique of political philosophy. This approach has not always been done well because the thinking of Marx scholars has too often been locked within the categories of political economy, but as a mode of reconstruction it is superior to the search for Marx's scattered and situated 'views' on these subjects. See my *Political Investigations*, ch. 5, 'Right and value: the unity of Hegel and Marx'.

5 The relation to Kant is ever present in Arendt's work. Arendt writes of Kant's 'paradoxical legacy . . . just as man comes of age and is declared autonomous, he is utterly debased'. She comments that this legacy is an accurate reflection of 'the antinomical structure of human being as it is situated in the world'. The splitting of the life of the mind into the distinct 'faculties' of thinking, willing and judging turns out to be one aspect of the antinomical structure of human beings as we are currently situated in the world. Kant recognises and helps to create one of modernity's major accomplishments, the autonomy of reason, but for Arendt he pays too big a price for it: the separation of reason into allegedly autonomous fields. *Essays in Understanding*, pp. 169–71. Cited in Kohn (1997: 163).

6 Ronald Beiner writes: 'It is not merely that the already completed

accounts of two mental faculties were to be supplemented by a yet-to-be provided third but, rather, that those two accounts themselves remain deficient without the promised synthesis in judging ... So we arrive at the threshold of Judging still in search of solutions to the basic problems that impelled Arendt to write *The Life of the Mind*' ('Interpretive Essay', in Arendt 1992: 89–90).

7 I find curious parallels between the structure of *The Life of the Mind* and Arendt's earlier work, *On Revolution*. In the latter, Arendt distinguished between three moments of the revolutionary tradition: the American, the French, and the 'lost treasure' of town hall and council democracy that has existed on the margins of every modern revolutionary movement. At first sight, it appears that Arendt is positive about the tradition of 1776, negative about the tradition of 1789 and finds the realisation of the revolutionary idea in the lost treasure of participatory democracy. On reflection, however, we find along with Arendt that the American revolutionary tradition has its own disabling contradictions (e.g. its prioritisation of private rights over rights of public participation); that the French revolutionary tradition represents a huge achievement despite the terror (especially its formulation of the 'constitution of liberty'); and that the 'lost treasure' of radical participatory democracy has far more problems than is apparent at first sight. Arendt finishes the text on this note when she calls the council system an 'aristocratic' form of government run by a self-constituting elite (Arendt 1988: 279–80). As her study of revolution unfolds, it becomes apparent that there is no 'pure' revolutionary tradition, no ideal form of actualisation, no formula for liberation from tyranny and the constitution of liberty that does not reinstate the perplexities of foundation and new beginnings. The underlying structure of *On Revolution*, then, is not 'dialectical', or rather is dialectical only in the sense that it is a study of the development of the idea of revolution as it dissolves and produces its various particularisations. The lesson Arendt drew, or seems to have drawn, is not to repudiate the modern revolutionary tradition but to retain our political judgement in the midst of its perplexities. See Arendt 1988.

8 For Ernst Junger, this negation of all existing standards was transmuted into the hope that the whole culture and texture of life might go down in 'storms of steel'. War appeared as the means of chastisement and purification in a corrupt age (Thomas Mann); as the great equaliser in class-ridden societies (Lenin); as the arena in which selflessness obliterates bourgeois egoism (Bakunin); as the site of the doomed man with no personal interest, no attachments, no property, not even a name of his own (Nechaev).

9 There are many interesting parallels still to be drawn between Hegel's analysis of the 'freedom of the void' and Arendt's analysis of the 'abyss of freedom' (Fine 2001a: 36–9, 100–19).

10 Primo Levi wrote of his desire to understand the Germans but nonetheless refused to meet the German chemist at Auschwitz for fear that

this encounter might prevent him from making 'the correct judgment'. In the Afterword of *If This is a Man* Levi declared his own equivocation thus: 'Perhaps one cannot, what is more one must not, understand what happened, because to understand is almost to justify . . . I cannot say I understand the Germans' (Levi 1995: 395–6). His fear was that understanding the Germans might lead to loss of judgement even though his purpose was to understand and judge at the same time.

11   Again there are interesting resemblances between Arendt's notion of understanding and that of Hegel. In the Preface to his *Philosophy of Right* Hegel famously comments: 'To comprehend what is, is the task of philosophy, for what is, is reason . . . If his [an individual's] theory . . . builds a world as it ought to be, then it certainly has an existence, but only within his opinions – a pliant medium in which the imagination can construct anything it pleases . . . this rational insight is the reconciliation with actuality which philosophy grants to those who have received the inner call to comprehend, to preserve their subjective freedom in the realm of the substantial and at the same time to stand with their subjective freedom . . . in what has being in and for itself' (Hegel 1991: 21–2).

12   Arendt's characterisation of the social sciences is overblown to the extent that an array of positions in the field has sought to face the tensions between facts and norms. I would rather see Arendt as providing a critique of positivist social science from within the parameters of social science.

Conclusion

1   A similar methodological error is to be found in other fields of social inquiry. For example, critical histories of the Labour party in the UK may construct an ideal of socialism which the Labour party has never fulfilled and represent its history as one betrayal after another of an ideal which exists only in the head of the critic and his or her fellow thinkers. This essentially idealist methodology displays no shortage of judgement but it cannot possibly understand the dynamics of the party.

2   For example, in my research on black workers in South Africa (Fine 1991), I explored how some workers struggled against all the odds for basic human rights in the apartheid workplace and how the winning of basic human rights brought with it new dilemmas caused by the legalisation of trade unions, the establishment of industrial courts and thence the ensconcing of labour rights in the constitution of the new South Africa. The movement between struggles for human rights and the institutionalisation of human rights is inherent in the phenomenon itself. This movement runs in both directions and in the case of more vulnerable workers institutionalisation may well precede the possibility of struggle.

3   For   example,   in   his   impassioned   polemic   against   existing

cosmopolitanism, Costas Douzinas establishes the 'cosmopolitanism to come', based on 'universal but absent principles beyond all law and finitude', as the position from which the law of the polis is judged and found wanting. The axiom of cosmopolitan justice he puts forward is that of justice to the other and respect for the singularity of the other. His cosmopolitan principle is that each singular being is a cosmos and that the other is a 'unique finite being that puts me in touch with infinite' otherness (Douzinas 2007). Rather than explore the dialectic between respect for the singularity of the other and respect for human rights, the one is simply opposed to the other and given its separate label.

BIBLIOGRAPHY

Adorno, Theodor (1990) *Negative Dialectics*, Routledge, London.

Agamben, Giorgio (1998) *Homo Sacer: sovereign power and bare life*, Stanford University Press, Stanford.

Agamben, Giorgio (2005) *State of Exception* (trans. Kevin Attell), Chicago University Press, Chicago.

Albrow, Martin (1996) *The Global Age*, Polity, Cambridge.

Anderson, Benedict (1983) *Imagined Communities: reflections on the origin and spread of nationalism*, Verso, London.

Apel, Karl-Otto (1997) 'Kant's "Toward Perpetual Peace" as Historical Prognosis from the Point of View of Moral Duty', pp. 79–110 in James Bohman and Matthias Lutz-Bachmann (eds), *Perpetual Peace: essays on Kant's cosmopolitan ideal*, MIT Press, Cambridge, MA.

Appiah, Kwame Anthony (1996) 'Cosmopolitan Patriots', pp. 21–9 in Joshua Cohen (ed.), *For Love of Country: debating the limits of patriotism*, Beacon, Boston. A longer version of this paper is in Pheng Cheah and Bruce Robbins (eds) (1998), *Cosmopolitics: thinking and feeling beyond the nation*, University of Minnesota Press, Minneapolis, pp. 91–114, and in *Critical Inquiry*, Spring 1997, 617–39.

Archibugi, Daniele (1995) 'Immanuel Kant, Cosmopolitan Law and Peace', *European Journal of International Relations*, 1, 4, 429–56.

Archibugi, Daniele (2000) 'Cosmopolitical Democracy', *New Left Review*, 4, 137–50.

Archibugi, Daniele (ed.) (2004a) *Cosmopolitics*, Verso, London.

Archibugi, Daniele (2004b) 'Cosmopolitical Democracy', pp. 1–15 in Daniele Archibugi (ed.), *Debating Cosmopolitics*, Verso, London.

Archibugi, Daniele (2004c) 'Cosmopolitan Guidelines for Humanitarian Intervention', *Alternatives: Global, Local, Political*, 29, 1, 1–22.

Archibugi, Daniele and Held, David (eds) (1995) *Cosmopolitan Democracy: an agenda for a new world order*, Polity, Cambridge.

Archibugi, Daniele *et al.* (eds) (1998) *Re-imagining Political Community: studies in cosmopolitan democracy*, Polity, Cambridge.

Arendt, Hannah (1958) *The Human Condition*, University of Chicago Press, Chicago.

Arendt, Hannah (1977a) *Between Past and Future*, Penguin, Harmondsworth.

Arendt, Hannah (1977b) *Eichmann in Jerusalem: A Report on the Banality of Evil*, Penguin, Harmondsworth.

Arendt, Hannah (1978a) *Jew as Pariah*, Grove Press, New York.

Arendt, Hannah (1978b) *The Life of the Mind*, Harcourt Brace Jovanovich, Orlando, FL.

Arendt, Hannah (1979) *The Origins of Totalitarianism*, Harcourt Brace, New York.

Arendt, Hannah (1988) *On Revolution*, Penguin, Harmondsworth.

Arendt, Hannah (1992) *Lectures on Kant's Political Philosophy* (ed. with an interpretive essay by Ronald Beiner), Chicago University Press, Chicago.

Arendt, Hannah (1994) *Essays in Understanding*, Harcourt Brace, New York.

Arendt, Hannah (2003) *Responsibility and Judgement* (ed. Jerome Kohn), Schocken, New York.

Arendt, Hannah and Jaspers, Karl (1992) *Hannah Arendt/Karl Jaspers: correspondence 1926–1969* (ed. Lotte Kohler and Han Saner), Harcourt Brace, New York.

Arendt, Hannah and McCarthy, Mary (1995) *Between Friends: the correspondence of Hannah Arendt and Mary McCarthy 1949–1975* (ed. Carol Brightman), Harcourt Brace, New York.

Aron, R. (1972) *Progress and Disillusion*, Penguin, Harmondsworth.

Baehr, Peter (2002) 'Identifying the Unprecedented: Hannah Arendt, totalitarianism and the critique of sociology', *American Sociological Review*, 67, 804–31.

Baehr, Peter (2004) 'Of Politics and Social Science: "totalitarianism" in the dialogue of David Riesman and Hannah Arendt', *European Journal of Political Theory*, 3, 2, 191–217.

Balibar, Étienne (2004) *We, The People of Europe? Reflections on Transnational Citizenship* (trans. James Swenson), Princeton University Press, Princeton.

Barnett, Michael (2003) 'Bureaucratising the Duty to Aid: the United Nations and the Rwandan genocide', pp. 174–191 in A. F. Lang, Jr. (ed.), *Just Intervention*, Georgetown University Press, Washington DC.

Bartelson, Jens (2001) *The Critique of the State*, Cambridge University Press, Cambridge.

Bataille, Georges (1990) *Literature and Evil*, Marion Boyers, London.

Baudrillard, Jean (2002) *The Spirit of Terrorism* (trans. Chris Turner), Verso, London.

Bauman, Zygmunt (1990) *Modernity and the Holocaust*, Polity, Cambridge.

Baynes, Kenneth (1997) 'Communitarian and Cosmopolitan Challenges to Kant's Conception of World Peace', pp. 219–234 in J. Bohman and M. Lutz-Bachmann (eds), *Perpetual Peace: essays on Kant's cosmopolitan ideal*, The MIT Press, London.

Beck, Ulrich (1998a) 'The Cosmopolitan Manifesto', *New Statesman*, 20, 38–50.

Beck, Ulrich (1998b) *Democracy Without Enemies*, Polity, Cambridge.

Beck, Ulrich (2000a) 'The Cosmopolitan Perspective: sociology of the second age of modernity', *British Journal of Sociology*, 51, 1, 79–105.

Beck, Ulrich (2000b) *The Brave New World of Work*, Polity, Cambridge.

Beck, Ulrich (2000c) *What is Globalization?*, Polity, Cambridge.

Beck, Ulrich (2002a) 'The Cosmopolitan Society and its Enemies', *Theory, Culture and Society*, 19, 1/2, 17–45.

Beck, Ulrich (2002b) 'The Terrorist Threat: world risk society revisited', *Theory, Culture and Society*, 19, 4, 39–55.

Beck, Ulrich (2003) 'Towards a New Critical Theory with a Cosmopolitan Intent', *Constellations*, 10, 4, 453–68.

Beck, Ulrich (2006a) *Cosmopolitan Vision*, Polity, Cambridge.

Beck, Ulrich (2006b) *Power in the Global Age*, Polity, Cambridge.

Beck, Ulrich and Sznaider, Natan (eds) (2006) *British Journal of Sociology*, special issue on cosmopolitan sociology, 57, 1.

Beck, Ulrich and Grande, Edgar (2007) 'Cosmopolitanism – Europe's Way Out of Crisis', *European Journal of Social Theory*, 10, 1, 67–85.

Beiner, Ronald (1983) *Political Judgment*, Methuen, London.

Beiner, Ronald (1994) 'Judging in a World of Appearances: a commentary on Hannah Arendt's unwritten finale', pp. 365–87 in Lewis and Sandra Hinchman (eds), *Hannah Arendt: critical essays*, State University of New York Press, Albany, NY.

Beiner, Ronald and Nedelsky, Jennifer (eds) (2001) *Judgment, Imagination and Politics: themes from Kant and Arendt*, Rowman and Littlefield Publishers, New York.

Beitz, Charles (1999) *Political Theory and International Relations*, Princeton University Press, Princeton.

Beitz, Charles (2000) 'Rawls's Law of Peoples', *Ethics*, 110, 669–96.

Bellamy, Alex (2005) 'Responsibility to Protector Trojan horse? The crisis in Darfur and humanitarian intervention after Iraq', *Ethics and International Affairs*, 19, 31–53.

Benhabib, Seyla (2002) *The Claims of Culture: equality and diversity in the global era*, Princeton University Press, Oxford.

Benhabib, Seyla (2004) *The Rights of Others: aliens, residents, and citizens*, Cambridge University Press, Cambridge.

Benjamin, Walter (1968) 'Theses on the Philosophy of History', pp. 255–66 in Hannah Arendt (ed.), *Illuminations*, Schocken, New York.

Berman, Paul (2004) *Terror and Liberalism*, WW Norton and Company, New York.

Bernstein, Richard (1996) *Hannah Arendt and the Jewish Question*, Polity, Cambridge.

Bernstein, Richard (2002) *Radical Evil: a philosophical interrogation*, Polity, Oxford.

Bobbitt, P. (2002) *The Shield of Achilles: war, peace and the course of history*, Penguin, London.

Bohman, James and Lutz-Bachmann, Matthias (eds) (1997) *Perpetual Peace: essays on Kant's cosmopolitan ideal*, The MIT Press, London.

Boon, Vivienne and Fine, Robert (eds) (2007) *European Journal of Social Theory*, special issue on cosmopolitanism: between past and future, 10, 1.

Booth, Ken (2001) 'Ten Flaws of Just Wars', pp. 314–324 in Ken Booth (ed.), *The Kosovo Tragedy: the human rights dimension*, Frank Cass, London.

Breckenridge, Carol and Pollock, Sheldon (eds) (2002) *Cosmopolitanism*, Duke University Press, Durham, NC and London.

Brown, Chris (2002) *Sovereignty, Rights and Justice: international political theory today*, Polity, Oxford.

Brown, Chris (2003) 'Selective Humanitarianism: in defence of inconsistency', pp. 31–50 in D. K. Chatterjee and D. E. Scheid (eds), *Ethics and Foreign Intervention*, Cambridge University Press, Cambridge.

Brown, Chris (2006) 'Kantian Cosmopolitan Law and the Idea of a Cosmopolitan Constitution', *History of Political Thought*, 27, 4, 661–84.

Browning, Christopher (1993) *Ordinary Men: Reserve Battalion 101 and the final solution in Poland*, Harper Perennial, New York.

Buchanan, Allen (2000) 'Rawls' Law of Peoples: rules for a vanished Westphalian world', *Ethics*, 110, 4, 697–721.

Buck-Morss, Susan (2002) *Dreamworld and Catastrophe: the passing of mass utopia in East and West*, MIT Press, Cambridge, MA.

Bull, Hedley (1992) *Hugo Grotius and International Relations*, Clarendon Press, Oxford.

Bull, Hedley (1995) *The Anarchical Society: a study of order in world politics*, Macmillan, Basingstoke.

Calhoun, Craig (2003) 'The Class Consciousness of Frequent Travellers: towards a critique of actually existing cosmopolitanism', pp. 86–109 in Steve Vertovec and Robin Cohen (eds) *Conceiving Cosmopolitanism*, Oxford University Press, Oxford.

Cassesse, Antonio (2001) *International Law*, Oxford University Press, Oxford.

Castells, Manuel (2000) *The Rise of the Network Society*, Blackwell, Oxford.

Cavallar, Georg (1999) *Kant and the Theory and Practice of International Right*, University of Wales Press, Cardiff.

Caverero, Adriana (1992) 'Equality and Sexual Difference: amnesia in political thought', pp. 32–47 in G. Bock and S. James (eds), *Beyond Equality and Difference: citizenship, feminist politics and female subjectivity*, Routledge, London.

Chandler, David (2003) 'International Justice', pp. 27–39 in Daniele Archibugi (ed.), *Debating Cosmopolitics*, Verso, London.

Cheah, Pheng and Robbins, Bruce (eds) (1998) *Cosmopolitics: thinking and feeling beyond the nation*, University of Minnesota Press, Minneapolis.

Chernilo, Daniel (2006a) 'Social Theory's Methodological Nationalism: myth and reality', *European Journal of Social Theory*, 9, 1, 5–22.

Chernilo, Daniel (2006b) 'Methodological Nationalism and its Critique' pp. 129–140 in G. Delanty and K. Kumar (eds), *The Sage Handbook of Nations and Nationalism*, Sage, London.

Chernilo, Daniel (2007a) 'A Quest for Universalism: re-assessing the nature of classical social theory's cosmopolitanism', *European Journal of Social Theory* 10, 1, 17–35.

Chernilo, Daniel (2007b) *A Social Theory of the Nation-State: beyond methodological nationalism*, Routledge, London.

Chernilo, Daniel (2007c) 'Universalismo y Cosmopolitismo en la Teoría de Jürgen Habermas', *Estudios Públicos*, 106 Otoño.

Chernilo, Daniel (2008a, forthcoming) 'Classical Sociology and the Nation-State: a re-interpretation', *Journal of Classical Sociology*, 8, 1.

Chernilo, Daniel (2008b, forthcoming) 'Talcott Parsons' Sociology of the Nation-State' in C. Hart (ed.), *Talcott Parsons: theories, developments and applications*.

Chernilo, Daniel (2008c, forthcoming) 'Cosmopolitanism and Sociology' in Bryan Turner (ed.), *The Blackwell Companion to Social Theory*, Blackwell, Oxford.

Chomsky, Noam (1999) *The New Military Humanism: lessons from Kosovo*, Pluto, London.

Cohen, Joshua (ed.) (1996) *For Love of Country: debating the limits of patriotism – Martha Nussbaum and respondents*, Beacon Press, Cambridge.

Cohen, Stanley (2001) *States of Denial: knowing about atrocities and suffering*, Polity, Cambridge.

Cohen, Jean (2004) 'Whose sovereignty? Empire versus international law', *Ethics and International Affairs*, 18, 3, 1–24.

Deak, Istvan (1993) 'Misjudgment at Nuremberg', *New York Review of Books*, 7 October 1993, 46–52.

Delanty, Gerard (2000) *Citizenship in a Global Age*, Open University Press, Buckingham.

Delanty, Gerard (2006a) 'Nationalism and Cosmopolitanism: the paradox of modernity', pp. 357–368 in G. Delanty and K. Kumar (eds), *Handbook of Nations and Nationalism*, Sage, London.

Delanty, Gerard (2006b) 'The Cosmopolitan Imagination: critical cosmopolitanism and social theory', *British Journal of Sociology*, 57, 1, 25–47.

Deleuze, Gilles and Guattari, Félix (1986) *Nomadology: the war machine* (trans. Brian Massumi), Semiotext(e), Paris.

d'Entrèves, Maurizio Passerin (2000) 'Arendt's theory of judgment', pp. 245–60 in Dana Villa (ed.), *The Cambridge Companion to Hannah Arendt*, Cambridge University Press, Cambridge

Derrida, Jacques (1994) *The Other Heading: reflections on today's Europe*, Indiana University Press, Bloomington.

Douglas, Lawrence (2001) *The Memory of Judgement: making law and history in the trials of the Holocaust*, Yale University Press, New Haven and London.

Douzinas, Costas (2000) *The End of Human Rights: critical legal thought at the end of the century*, Hart, Oxford.

Douzinas, Costas (2007) *Human Rights and Empire: the political philosophy of cosmopolitanism*, Routledge-Cavendish, London.

Doyle, Michael (1993) 'Liberalism and International Relations', pp. 173–204 in R. Beiner and W. Booth (eds.), *Kant and Political Philosophy: the contemporary legacy*, Yale University Press, New Haven.

Durkheim, Emile (1992) *Professional Ethics and Civic Morals* (trans. Cornelia Brookfield), Routledge, London.

Eleftheriadis, Pavlos (2003), 'Cosmopolitan Law', *European Law Journal*, 9, 241–63.

Elias, Norbert (1997), *The Germans: power struggles and the development of habitus in the nineteenth and twentieth centuries* (ed. Michael Schröter, trans. Eric Dunning and Stephen Mennell), Polity, Cambridge.

Elliott, L. and Cheeseman, G. (2002) 'Cosmopolitan Theory, Militaries and the Deployment of Force', Working Paper, University of Canberra, Department of International Relations.

Ellis, Elizabeth (2005) *Kant's Politics: provisional theory for an uncertain world*, Yale University Press, New Haven and London.

Falk, Richard (1998) *Law in an Emerging Global Village: a post-Westphalian perspective*, Transnational, New York.

Falk, Richard (1999) 'Kosovo, World Order, and the Future of International Law', *American Journal of International Law*, 93, 4, 847–57.

Ferrara, Alessandro (1999) *Justice and Judgment: the rise and prospect of the judgment model in contemporary political philosophy*, Sage, London.

Ferrara, Alessandro (2007) 'Political Cosmopolitanism and Judgment' in V. Boon and R. Fine (eds) (2007), 'Cosmopolitanism: between past and future', *European Journal of Social Theory*, 10, 1, 53–66.

Fine, Robert (1991) *Beyond Apartheid: labour and liberation in South Africa*, Pluto, London.

Fine, Robert (1994a) 'The New Nationalism and Democracy: a critique of *pro patria*', *Democratization*, 1, 3, 423–43.

Fine, Robert (1994b) 'The Rule of Law and Muggletonian Marxism: the perplexities of Edward Thompson', *Journal of Law and Society*, 21, 2, 193–213.

Fine, Robert (1997) 'Civil society, enlightenment and critique', pp. 7–28 in Robert Fine and Shirin Rai (eds), *Civil Society, Democratic Perspectives*, Frank Class, London.

Fine, Robert (2000) 'Crimes Against Humanity: Hannah Arendt and the Nuremberg debates', *European Journal of Social Theory*, 3, 3, 293–311.

Fine, Robert (2001a) *Political Investigations: Hegel, Marx, Arendt*, Routledge, London.

Fine, Robert (2001b), 'Understanding Evil: Arendt and the final solution', pp. 131–50 in Maria Pia Lara (ed.) *Rethinking Evil: contemporary perspectives*, University of California Press, Los Angeles.

Fine, Robert (2002) *Democracy and the Rule of Law: Marx's critique of the legal form*, Blackburn Press, NJ.

Fine, Robert (2003a) 'Kant's Theory of Cosmopolitanism and Hegel's Critique', *Philosophy and Social Criticism*, 29, 6, 609–30.

Fine, Robert (2003b) 'Taking the "ism" out of Cosmopolitanism', *European Journal of Social Theory*, 6, 4, 451–70.

Fine, Robert (2005) 'Cosmopolitanism: a research agenda', pp. 242–53 in Gerard Delanty (ed.), *The Handbook of Contemporary European Social Theory*, Routledge, London.

Fine, Robert (2006a) 'The Charge of Evil and Contemporary Political Belonging', pp. 149–60 in Nira Yuval-Davis, Kalpana Kannabiran and Ulrike M. Vieten (eds), *Situating Contemporary Politics of Belonging*, Sage, London.

Fine, Robert (2006b) 'Cosmopolitanism and Violence', special issue of *British Journal of Sociology* ed. Ulrich Beck and Natan Sznaider, 57, 1, 49–67.

Fine, Robert (2008, forthcoming) 'Judgment and the Reification of the Faculties: a reconstructive reading of Arendt's *Life of the Mind*', *Philosophy and Social Criticism*, special issue on Judgement, ed. Alessandro Ferrara.

Fine, Robert and Hirsh, David (2000) 'The Decision to Commit a Crime Against Humanity', in Margaret Archer and Jonathan Tritter (eds), *Rational Choice Theory: resisting colonisation*, Routledge, London.

Fine, Robert and Chernilo, Daniel (2003) 'Classes and Nations in Recent Historical Sociology', pp. 235–50 in Gerard Delanty and Engin Isin (eds), *Handbook of Historical Sociology*, Sage, London.

Fine, Robert and Cohen, Robin (2003) 'Four Cosmopolitan Moments', pp. 137–64 in Steven Vertovec and Robin Cohen (eds), *Conceiving Cosmopolitanism*, Oxford University Press, Oxford.

Fine, Robert and Smith, William (2003) 'Jürgen Habermas' Theory of Cosmopolitanism', *Constellations*, 10, 4, 469–87.

Fine, Robert and Chernilo, Daniel (2004) 'Between Past and Future: the equivocations of the new cosmopolitanism', *Studies in Law, Politics, and Society*, 31, 25–44.

Fine, Robert and Vazquez, Rolando (2006) 'Freedom and Right in Modern Society: reading Hegel's *Philosophy of Right*', pp. 241–53 in Michael Freeman (ed.), *Law and Sociology: Current Legal Issues* vol. 8, Oxford University Press, Oxford.

Finkielkraut, Alain (1992) *Remembering in Vain*, Columbia, New York.

Finkielkraut, Alain (2001) *In the Name of Humanity: reflections on the twentieth century*, Random House, London.

Flikschuh, Katrin (2000) *Kant and Modern Political Philosophy*, Cambridge University Press, Cambridge.

Foucault, Michel (1973) *Madness and Civilisation: a history of madness in the age of reason*, Vintage, New York.

Gerth, H. H. and Mills, C. Wright (1991) *From Max Weber: essays in sociology*, Routledge, London.

Giddens, Anthony (1973) *The Class Structure of Advanced Societies*, Hutchinson, London.

Giddens, Anthony (1985) *The Nation-State and Violence*, Polity, Cambridge.

Gorz, Andre (1989) *Critique of Economic Reason*, Verso, London.

Habermas, Jürgen (1988) *Legitimation Crisis*, Polity, Cambridge.

Habermas, Jürgen (1993) *Justification and Application*, (trans. Ciaran Cronin), Polity, Cambridge.

Habermas, Jürgen (1996) *Between Facts and Norms: contributions to a discourse theory of law and democracy*, Polity, Oxford.

Habermas, Jürgen (1997) 'Kant's Idea of Perpetual Peace, with the Benefit of Two Hundred Years' Hindsight', pp. 113–153 in J. Bohman and M. Lutz-Bachmann (eds), *Perpetual Peace: essays on Kant's cosmopolitan ideal*, The MIT Press, London.

Habermas, Jürgen (1998) *Inclusion of the Other: studies in political theory*, Polity, Cambridge.

Habermas, Jürgen (1999a) 'Bestiality and Humanity: a war on the border between legality and morality', *Constellations* 6, 3, 263–72.

Habermas, Jürgen (1999b) 'Kant's Idea of Perpetual Peace: at two hundred years' historical remove' in J. Habermas, *The Inclusion of the Other: studies in political theory*, The MIT Press, Cambridge.

Habermas, Jürgen (2001a) *The Postnational Constellation: political essays* (ed. Max Pensky), Polity, Cambridge.

Habermas, Jürgen (2001b) 'Why Europe Needs a Constitution', *New Left Review*, 11, 5–26.

Habermas, Jürgen (2002) 'Letter to America', *The Nation*, 16 December 2002, available at http://www.thenation.com/doc/20021216/habermas.

Habermas, Jürgen (2003) 'Interpreting the Fall of a Monument', *Constellations*, 10, 3, 364–70.

Habermas, Jürgen (2004) 'America and the World: a conversation with Jürgen Habermas, with Eduardo Mendieta', *Logos*, 3, 3, 101–22.

Habermas, Jürgen (2006) *The Divided West* (ed. and trans. Ciaran Cronin), Polity, Cambridge.

Habermas, Jürgen and Derrida, Jacques (2003a) *Philosophy in a Time of Terror: dialogues with Jürgen Habermas and Jacques Derrida* (ed. Giovanna Borradori), University of Chicago, Chicago.

Habermas, Jürgen and Derrida, Jacques (2003b) 'February 15, or What Binds Europeans Together: a plea for a common foreign policy, beginning in the core of Europe', *Constellations*, 10, 3, 291–7.

Hardt, Michael and Negri, Antonio (2000) *Empire*, Harvard University Press, Cambridge, MA.

Hegel, Georg (1956) *The Philosophy of History*, Dover Publications, Toronto and London.

Hegel, Georg (1975) *Lectures in the Philosophy of World History: introduction* (trans. H. B. Nisbet), Cambridge University Press, Cambridge.

Hegel, Georg (1991) *Philosophy of Right* (ed. Allen W. Wood, trans. H. B. Nisbet), Cambridge University Press, Cambridge.

Heidegger, Martin (1976) 'Letter on Humanism', pp. 189–242 in David Krell (ed.), *Basic Writings*, Harper and Row, San Francisco.

Held, David (1995a) *Democracy and the Global Order*, Polity, Cambridge.

Held, David (1995b) 'Democracy and the New International Order', pp. 96–120 in D. Archibugi and D. Held (eds), *Cosmopolitan Democracy*, Polity, Cambridge.

Held, David (2004) *Global Covenant*, Polity, Cambridge.

Held, David and McGrew, Anthony (eds) (2002) *Governing Globalization*, Polity, Oxford.

Hill, Jason (2000) *Becoming a Cosmopolitan*, Rowman and Littlefield, Oxford.

Hirsh, David (2003) *Law Against Genocide*, Glasshouse Press, London.

Hirsh, David (2006) 'Cosmopolitan Law: agency and narrative' in Michael Freeman (ed) *Law and Sociology*, Oxford University Press, Oxford.

Hobbes, Thomas (1996) *Leviathan*, Cambridge University Press, Cambridge.

Hobsbawm, Eric (1994) *Nations and Nationalism Since 1780*, Cambridge University Press, Cambridge.

Hoffe, Otfried (2006) *Kant's Cosmopolitan Theory of Law and Peace*, Cambridge University Press, Cambridge.

Hollinger, David (2001) 'Not Universalists, Not Pluralists: the new cosmopolitans find their own way', *Constellations*, 8, 2, 236–48.

Holzgrefe, J. L. (2003) 'The Humanitarian Intervention Debate', pp. 15–52 in J. L. Holzgrefe and R. O. Keohane (eds), *Humanitarian Intervention: ethical, legal and political dilemmas*, Cambridge University Press, Cambridge.

Honneth, Axel (1997) 'Is Universalism a Moral Trap? The Presuppositions and Limits of a Politics of Human Rights' in J. Bohman and M. Lutz-Bachmann (eds) *Perpetual Peace: essays on Kant's cosmopolitan ideal*, The MIT Press, London.

Ignatieff, M. (1999) *The Warrior's Honor: ethnic war and the modern conscience*, Vintage, London.

Ignatieff, Michael (2000) *Virtual War*, Chatto and Windus, London.

International Commission on Intervention and State Sovereignty (2001) *The Responsibility to Protect*, International Development Research Centre, Ottawa. Available at http://www.iciss.ca/report-en.asp

Jaspers, Karl (1961) *The Question of German Guilt*, Capricorn, New York.

Jaspers, Karl (2006) 'Who Should Have Tried Eichmann?', *Journal of International Criminal Justice*, 4, 4, 853–8.

Joas, Hans (2003) *War and Modernity Studies in the History of Violence*, Polity, Cambridge.

Kagan, Robert (2003) *Paradise and Power: America and Europe in the new world order*, Atlantic Books, London.

Kahn, Paul (2000) 'American Hegemony and International Law', *Chicago Journal of International Law*, 2, 1–18.

Kaldor, Mary (2001) *New and Old Wars: organised violence in a global era*, Polity, Cambridge.

Kaldor, Mary (2003) *Global Civil Society: an answer to war*, Polity, Oxford.

Kant, Immanuel (1965) *The Metaphysical Elements of Justice*, part 1 of *The Metaphysics of Morals* (trans. John Ladd), Bobbs-Merrill, Indianapolis.

Kant, Immanuel (1970) in *Kant: political writings* (ed. and intro. Hans Reiss), Cambridge University Press, Cambridge.

Kant, Immanuel (1987) *Critique of Judgment* (trans. Werner S. Pluhar), Hackett Publishing Company, Cambridge.

Kant, Immanuel (1991) *Kant: political writings* (ed. Hans Reiss), Cambridge University Press, Cambridge.

Kant, Immanuel (1996) *The Metaphysics of Morals* (ed. and trans. Mary Gregor), Cambridge University Press, Cambridge.

Kedourie, Elie (1993) *Nationalism*, Blackwell, Oxford.

Kirchheimer, Otto (1969) *Political Justice*, Princeton University Press, Princeton.

Koffman, Eleanor (2007) 'Figures of the Cosmopolitan: privileged nationals and national outsiders', pp. 239–256 in Chris Rumford (ed) *Cosmopolitanism and Europe*, Liverpool: Liverpool University Press.

Kohn, Jerome (1997) 'Evil and Plurality: Hannah Arendt's way to *The Life of the Mind I*', pp. 147–178 in Larry May and Jerome Kohn (eds), *Hannah Arendt: twenty years later*, MIT Press, Cambridge, MA.

Koskenniemi, Martti (2002) 'Between Impunity and Show Trials', *6 Max Planck Yearbook of United Nations*, 1.

Krisch, Nico (2002) 'Legality, Morality and the Dilemma of Humanitarian Interventions after Kosovo', *European Journal of International Law*, 13, 1, 323–35.

Krisch, Nico (2004) 'Imperial International Law', *Global Law Working Paper*, Hauser Global Law School Program. Available at www. nyulawglobal.org/workingpapers/detail/GLWP_0104.htm.

Kristeva, Julia (1991) *Strangers to Ourselves*, Columbia University Press, New York.

Kumm, Mattias (2004) 'The Legitimacy of International Law: a constitutionalist framework of analysis', *European Journal of International Law*, 15, 5, 907–31.

Kuper, Andrew (2000) 'Rawlsian Global Justice: beyond *The Law of Peoples* to a cosmopolitan law of peoples', *Political Theory*, 28, 5, 640–74.

Kymlicka, Will (1995) *Multicultural Citizenship: a liberal theory of minority rights*, Clarendon Press, Oxford.

Kymlicka, Will (2001) *Contemporary Political Philosophy: an introduction*, Oxford University Press, Oxford.

Lang, Berel (1997) 'Strategies of Deception: the composition of Heidegger's silence', pp.1–18 in A. Milchman and A. Rosenberg (eds), *Martin Heidegger and the Holocaust*, Humanities Press, Atlantic Highlands, NJ.

Lara, Maria Pia (2007) 'Kant's Concept of Popular Sovereignty', working paper, Dept. of Philosophy, Universidad Autónoma Metropolitana, Mexico.

Lefort, Claude (1986) *The Political Forms of Modern Society*, MIT Press, Cambridge, MA.

Levi, Primo (1995) *If This is a Man*, Abacus, London.

Lévi-Strauss, Claude (1983) *Structural Anthropology* vol. 2, University of Chicago Press, Chicago.

Levy, Daniel and Sznaider, Natan (2002) 'The Holocaust and the Formation of Cosmopolitan Memory', *European Journal of Social Theory*, 5, 1, 87–106.

Linklater, Andrew (1998) *The Transformation of Political Community: ethical foundations of the post-Westphalian era*, Polity, Oxford.

Löwith, Karl (1967) *From Hegel to Nietzsche*, Anchor, New York.

Lupel, Adam (2004) 'Democratizing Global Governance: popular sovereignty and transnational politics', *American Political Science Association 100th Annual Meeting*, Chicago, Illinois, 2–5 September.

Lutz-Bachmann, Matthias (1997) 'Kant's Idea of Peace and the Philosophical Conception of a World Republic', pp. 59–78 in James Bohman and Matthias Lutz-Bachmann (eds) (1997), *Perpetual Peace: essays on Kant's cosmopolitan ideal*, MIT Press, Cambridge, MA.

Lyotard, Jean-François (1988) *The Differend: phrases in dispute*, Manchester University Press, Manchester.

McCarthy, Thomas (1997) 'On the Idea of a Reasonable Law of Peoples', pp. 201–17 in J. Bohman and M. Lutz-Bachmann (eds), *Perpetual Peace: essays on Kant's cosmopolitan ideal*, The MIT Press, London.

McGoldrick, Dominic (2004) *From 9–11 to the Iraq War 2003: international law in an age of complexity*, Hart, Oxford.

Makkreel, Rudolf (1994) *Imagination and Interpretation in Kant: the hermeneutical import of the critique of judgment*, University of Chicago Press, Chicago.

Mann, Michael (2005) *The Dark Side of Democracy: explaining ethnic cleansing*, Cambridge University Press, Cambridge.

Marcuse, Herbert (1979) *Reason and Revolution: Hegel and the rise of social theory*, Beacon, Boston.

Marrus, Michael (ed.) (1997) *The Nuremberg War Crimes Trial 1945–46: a documentary history*, Bedford Books, Boston.

Martins, Herminio (1974) 'Time and Theory in Sociology', pp. 194–246 in John Rex (ed.), *Approaches to Sociology*, Routledge and Kegan Paul, London.

May, Larry (2005) *Crimes Against Humanity: a normative account*, Cambridge University Press, Cambridge.

May, Larry (2006) 'Crimes Against Humanity' *Ethics and International Relations*, 20, 3.

Mehta, Uday Singh (1999) *Liberalism and Empire: a study in nineteenth century British liberal thought*, University of Chicago Press, Chicago.

Meinecke, Friedrich (1977) *The Age of German Liberation: 1795–1815*, University of California Press, Berkeley.

Mertens, Thomas (1996) 'Cosmopolitanism and Citizenship: Kant against Habermas' *European Journal of Philosophy*, 4, 3, 328–47.

Michelman, Frank (2001) 'Morality, Identity, and "Constitutional Patriotism"', *Ratio Juris*, 14, 3, 253–271.

Neiman, Susan (2001) 'Theodicy in Jerusalem', pp. 65–90 in Steven Ascheim (ed.), *Hannah Arendt in Jerusalem*, University of California Press, Berkeley.

Neiman, Susan (2002) *Evil in Modern Thought: an alternative history of philosophy*, Princeton University Press, Princeton.

Neumann, Franz (1942) *Behemoth: the structure and practice of national socialism*, Gollanz, London.

Nietzsche, Friedrich (1969a) *The Will to Power*, Vintage, New York.

Nietzsche, Friedrich (1969b) *The Genealogy of Morals* (trans. Walter Kaufmann and R. J. Hollingdale), Vintage, New York.

Norrie, Alan (2006) 'Justice and The Slaughter-Bench: the problem of war guilt in Arendt and Jaspers',working paper, School of Law, King's College University of London.

Nussbaum, Martha (1991) 'Kant and Stoic Cosmopolitanism', *Journal of Political Philosophy*, 1, 1–25.

Nussbaum, Martha (1997) 'Kant and Cosmopolitanism', pp. 25–58 in Bohman and Lutz-Bachmann (eds), *Perpetual Peace: essays on Kant's cosmopolitan ideal*, The MIT Press, London.

Nussbaum, Martha (2002) *For Love of Country: debating the limits of patriotism* (ed. Joshua Cohen), Beacon Press, Boston.

Oliver, Kelly (ed.) (1993) *Ethics, Politics and Difference in Julia Kristeva's Writings*, Routledge, London.

O'Neill, Onora (2000) *Bounds of Justice*, Cambridge University Press, Cambridge.

Ossewaarde, Marinus (2007) 'Cosmopolitanism and the Society of Strangers', *Current Sociology*, 55, 3, 367–88.

Pagden, Anthony (2000) 'Stoicism, Cosmopolitanism and the Legacy of European Imperialism', *Constellations*, 7, 1, 3–22.

Pogge, Thomas (2001) 'Rawls on International Justice', *The Philosophical Quarterly*, 51, 203, 246–53.

Postel, D. (2002) 'Letter to America: an interview with Jürgen Habermas', *The Nation*, available at www.globalpolicy.org/security/issues/iraq/attack/2002/1216jurgen.htm.

Postone, Moishe (2006) 'History and Helplessness: mass mobilization and contemporary forms of anticapitalism', *Public Culture*, 18,1, 93–110.

Rabinbach, Anson (1997) *In the Shadow of Catastrophe: German intellectuals between apocalypse and enlightenment*, University of California Press, Berkeley.

Rancière, Jacques (2006) 'Who is the Subject of the Rights of Man?', available at www.16beavergroup.org/mtarchive/archives/001879print.html.

Rawls, John (1999) *The Law of Peoples*, Harvard University Press, London.

Rawls, John (2001) *Justice as Fairness: a restatement*, Harvard University Press, London.

Reeves, Eric (2005) 'Darfur in the Deepening Shadow of Auschwitz, Bosnia, Cambodia, Rwanda', available at www.sudanreeves.org/Sections-article531-p1.html.

Reiss, Hans (1991) 'Introduction', pp. 1–40 in *Kant: political writings*, Cambridge University Press, Cambridge.

Robertson, Geoffrey (2006) *Crimes Against Humanity: the struggle for global justice*, Penguin, Harmondsworth.

Rodinson, M. (1972) *Marxism and the Moslem World* (trans. Michael Pallis), Zed Press, London.

Rosales, José María (2001) *Patriotismo Constitucional: Dolf Sternberger* (trans. Luis Villar Borda), Universidad Externado de Colombia, Bogota.

Rose, Gillian (1996) *Mourning Becomes the Law: philosophy and representation*, Cambridge University Press, Cambridge.

Rose, Jacqueline (2005) *The Question of Zion*, Princeton University Press, Princeton.

Rosenau, James (2002) 'Governance in a New Global Order', pp. 70–87 in David Held and Anthony McGrew (eds), *Governing Globalization*, Polity, Oxford.

Roth, J. and Berenbaum, M. (1989) *Holocaust: religious and philosophical implications*, Paragon House, New York.

Roth, K. (2004) 'War in Iraq: not a humanitarian intervention', *Human Rights Watch*, available at http://hrw.org/wr2k4/download/3.pdf.

Salehi, Fariba (2002) *Postmodernity and the Decline of the Nation-State*, London University Press, London.

Salter, Michael (1999) 'Neo-facist Legal Theory on Trial: an interpretation of Carl Schmitt's defence at Nuremberg from the perspective of Franz Neumann's critical theory of law', *Res Publica*, 5, 2, 161–194.

Sands, Philippe (2006) *Lawless World: making and breaking global rules*, Penguin, Harmondsworth.

Sands, Philippe (ed.) (2003) *From Nuremberg to the Hague: the future of international criminal justice*, Cambridge University Press, Cambridge.

Schlereth, Thomas (1997) *The Cosmopolitan Ideal in Enlightenment Thought: its form and function in the ideas of Franklin, Hume and Voltaire*, University of Notre Dame Press, Notre Dame.

Schluchter, Wolfgang (1996) *Paradoxes of Modernity: culture and conduct in the theory of Max Weber*, Stanford University Press, Stanford.

Schmitt, Carl (1997) *The Concept of the Political* (trans. George Schwab), University of Chicago Press, Chicago.

Schmitt, Carl (2003) *The Nomos of the Earth in the International Law of the Jus Publicum Europaeum* (trans. G. L. Ulmen), Telos Press, New York.

Shue, H. (2003) 'Bombing to Rescue? NATO's 1999 Bombing of Serbia' in D. K. Chatterjee and D. E. Scheid (eds), *Ethics and Foreign Intervention*, Cambridge University Press, Cambridge.

Smelser, Neil (1997) *Problematics of Sociology*, University of California Press, Berkeley and Los Angeles.

Smith, William (2007a, forthcoming) 'Anticipating a Cosmopolitan Future: the case of humanitarian military intervention', *International Politics*, 44, 1, 72–89.

Smith, William (2007b) 'Cosmopolitan Citizenship: virtue, irony, and worldliness', *European Journal of Social Theory*, 10, 1, 37–52.

Smith, William (2007c) 'Reclaiming the Revolutionary Spirit: Arendt on civil disobedience', working paper, University of Dundee.

Smith, William and Fine, Robert (2004) 'Kantian Cosmopolitanism Today: John Rawls and Jürgen Habermas on Immanuel Kant's *Foedus Pacificum*', *Kings College Law Journal*, 15, 1, 5–22.

Sohn-Rethel, Alfred (1978) *Intellectual and Manual Labour: a critique of epistemology* (trans. Martin Sohn-Rethel), Macmillan, London.

Spivak, Gayatri (1996) *The Spivak Reader* (ed. Donna Landry and Gerald MacLean), Routledge, New York and London.

Strange, Susan (1999) 'The West-Failure System', *Review of International Studies*, 25 (1999), 345–54.

Taguieff, Pierre-André (2005) *Preachers of Hatred: an interview with Pierre-André Taguieff*, available at www.zionism-israel.com/ezine/New_Antizionism.htm.

Taylor, Charles (1994) *Multiculturalism: examining the politics of recognition* (ed. and intro. Amy Gutmann), Princeton University Press, Princeton.

Teubner, Günther (2004) 'Societal Constitutionalism: alternatives to state-centred constitutional theory', pp. 3–28 in Christian Joerges *et al.* (eds), *Transnational Governance and Constitutionalism*, Hart Publishing, Portland.

Toulmin, Stephen (1992) *Cosmopolis: the hidden agenda of modernity*, University of Chicago Press, Chicago.

Traverso, Enzo (2003) *The Origins of Nazi Violence*, New York, The New Press.

Tuck, Richard (2001) *The Rights of War and Peace: political thought and the international order from Grotius to Kant*, Oxford University Press, Oxford.

Turner, B. S. (2006) 'Classical Sociology and Cosmopolitanism: a critical defence of the social', *British Journal of Sociology*, 57, 1, 133–55.

Turner, Charles (2004) 'Jürgen Habermas: European or German?', *European Journal of Political Theory*, 3, 3, 293–314.

Urbinati, Nadia (2003) 'Can Cosmopolitical Democracy be Democratic?', pp. 71–4 in Daniele Archibugi (ed.), *Debating Cosmopolitcs*, Verso, London.

Urry, John (2000) *Sociology Beyond Societies: mobilities for the twenty-first century*, Routledge, London.

Urry, John (2002) 'The Global Complexities of September 11th', *Theory, Culture and Society*, 19, 4, 57–69.

Varouxakis, Georgios (2006) '"Patriotism", "Cosmopolitanism" and "Humanity" in Victorian Thought', *European Journal of Political Theory*, 5, 1, 100–18.

Vertovec, Steven and Cohen, Robin (eds) (2003) *Conceiving Cosmopolitanism: theory, context and practice*, Oxford University Press, Oxford.

Villa, Dana (1997) 'The Banality of Philosophy: Arendt on Heidegger and Eichmann', pp. 179–96 in Larry May and Jerome Kohn (eds), *Hannah Arendt: twenty years later*, MIT Press, Cambridge, MA.

Villa, Dana (1999) *Politics, Philosophy, Terror: essays in the thought of Hannah Arendt*, Princeton University Press, Princeton.

Wagner, Peter (1994) *A Sociology of Modernity, Liberty and Discipline*, Routledge, London and New York.

Wagner, Peter (2001) *Theorising Modernity*, Sage, London.

Wagner, Peter (2006) 'Social Theory And Political Philosophy', pp. 25–36 in Gerard Delanty (ed.), *Handbook of Contemporary European Social Theory*, Routledge, London.

Walzer, Michael (1995) *Towards a Global Civil Society*, Berghahn, Providence, Rhode Island.

Walzer, Michael (2000) *Just and Unjust Wars*, Basic Books, New York.

Webster, Frank (2002), *Theories of the Information Society*, London, Routledge.

Wellmer, Albrecht (2001) 'Hannah Arendt on Judgment: the unwritten doctrine of reason', pp. 165–182 in Ronald Beiner and Jennifer Nedelsky (eds), *Judgment, Imagination and Politics: themes from Kant and Arendt*, Rowman and Littlefield, New York.

Wheeler, Nicholas (2000) *Saving Strangers: humanitarian intervention in international society*, Oxford University Press, Oxford.

Young, Iris Marion (2007) *Global Challenges: war, self determination and responsibility for justice*, Polity, Cambridge.

Young-Bruehl, Elisabeth (2006) *Why Arendt Matters*, Yale University Press, New Haven.

Zin, Howard (2004) 'Of Paradise and Power', *Znet*, 9 February.

Zizek, Slavoj (2005) 'The Obscenity of Human Rights: violence as symptom', available at http://www.lacan.com/zizviol.htm.

Zolo, Danilo (1997) *Cosmopolis: prospects for world government*, Polity, Cambridge.

Zolo, Danilo (1999) 'A Cosmopolitan Philosophy of International Law? A Realist Approach', *Ratio Juris*, 12, 4, 429–44.

Zolo, Danilo (2002) *Invoking Humanity: war, law and global order*, Continuum, London.

INDEX